ROAD TO
RELATIONSHIP

PRAYING THE WORD | THE GOSPELS + ACTS

Copyright © 2024 by Riley Martin
The Road to Relationship – The Gospels + Acts
Riley Martin

Paperback ISBN: 979-8-9860083-5-6

All rights reserved. No portion of this book may be reproduced in any form without permission from Riley Martin.

Cover Design by Dallas Cole

Printed in the United States of America

CONTENTS

Foreword……………………………………………3

Introduction…………………………………………5

Matthew ……………………………………………9

Mark ………………………………………………..79

Luke ………………………………………………115

John ………………………………………………165

Acts ………………………………………………205

FOREWORD

On October 31, 1517, Martin Luther posted his *Ninety-five Theses* on the church door in Wittenberg, Germany. One of his statements was, "To be a Christian without prayer is no more possible than to be alive without breathing." This bold move by Martin Luther was one of the catalysts for the Protestant Reformation. Martin Luther discerned in his generation a prayerlessness amongst laity and believers alike. This lack of prayer was causing people to trust more in organization, politics, religion, and the arm of flesh rather than in a faithful, omniscient, omnipresent King of kings and Lord of lords. For whatever reason, people overcomplicated and/or undervalued prayer and drifted away from an intimate, consistent, and familiar personal relationship with God, resulting in a church and believers who were powerless and perfunctory.

In 1948, during Winston Churchill's speech to the British House of Commons, he declared, "Those that fail to learn from history are doomed to repeat it."

Here we are in 2023–2024, which is, without a doubt, the greatest hour of the church. We are a generation whose spiritual DNA is laced with prophetic promises. We must not repeat the spiritual failures of past church generations. We must quickly learn the education Martin Luther revealed in 1517 that a prayerful people will be a powerful people. We must refuse to paralyze our role in the kingdom of God by majoring on talents, programs, performances, and productions while minoring on the power-producing weapon of prayer. We must reject the form of godliness found in a Christianity that is proficient in word but void in the demonstration of the Spirit that flows freely out of the depthless rivers of prayer. Our personal Kingdom development and increase will be determined by our relationship with God. We can't go further in the Kingdom or deeper in the Spirit than we are willing to go in prayer.

Thankfully, in every generation God raises up a voice of one crying in the wilderness to prepare the way of the Lord. Pastor Riley Martin's book, *Prayers in the*

Gospels + Acts, is a clarion call in our generation to return to the true source of everything in the kingdom of God—prayer.

Charles G. Robinette
International Evangelist
Author of *Radically Apostolic*

INTRODUCTION

At last, the Road to Relationship has led us to the cross. It can be said that everything in the Old Testament points toward the cross, and everything after the Gospels looks back to the cross. It is the culmination of all the law and prophets. Jesus is the fulfillment of the law and the prophets. In these prayers, we get to see the life of Jesus—fully God and fully man—living and breathing among humanity.

Our first and foremost example is Jesus Christ. He then gave the keys of the Kingdom to Peter and the Apostles. Through the *Road to Relationship – The Gospels + Acts*, we learn to pray the life of Jesus and the first Christians. From the Lord's Prayer and every parable taught by Jesus to the establishment and expansion of the early church, engaging in these prayers means inviting the Kingdom into your daily existence. I pray that through this volume you grow closer to the mighty God who became flesh and dwelt among us. His name is Jesus.

MATTHEW

Matthew 3:2–3, NKJV
And saying, "Repent, for the kingdom of heaven is at hand!" For this is he who was spoken of by the prophet Isaiah, saying: "The voice of one crying in the wilderness: 'Prepare the way of the LORD; make His paths straight.'"

This passage introduces John the Baptist, the forerunner of Jesus Christ. His message was simple: "Repent, for the kingdom of heaven is at hand." Repentance is the first step in our relationship with God and should be a part of our prayer every day.

The passage follows up with a prophecy: "Prepare ye the way of the Lord, make his paths straight" (Matthew 3:3). Every minister and believer of the gospel should pray this prayer. It helps us tap into kingdom prayers and actions during the course of each day.

God, I repent before you. Cleanse me today, Lord. But I also ask that you will allow me to prepare the way for your second coming. Help me to make your paths straight in both word and deed everywhere I go.

Matthew 4:3–4

And when the tempter came to him, he said, If thou be the Son of God, command that these stones be made bread. But he answered and said, It is written, Man shall not live by bread alone, but by every word that proceedeth out of the mouth of God.

This is the first temptation of Jesus in the wilderness. Notice the temptation came at the end of Jesus' forty-day fast. This reveals one of the enemy's most-used tactics: he will tempt you at your weakest point. He often comes at the end of a long period of sacrifice, after a time of ministering, or anytime you've just poured yourself out to God and others. Jesus exampled the correct response to Satan's temptation when he quoted the Word of God.

I come against temptation in my life today. I pray that your Word would be my response to every temptation of the enemy.

Matthew 4:10
Then saith Jesus unto him, Get thee hence, Satan: for it is written, Thou shalt worship the Lord thy God, and him only shalt thou serve.

The narrative of the life of Jesus acts as a model for a believer's life. This interaction between Jesus and Satan is beneficial to one's prayer life. In this passage, Jesus showed believers how to respond to Satan.

First, the enemy will attempt to use the Word of God against you. Second, Satan is a liar and has been from the beginning. Not only is he a liar, but he is a clever one. He will twist God's words to make you believe they mean something other than what God intended. Jesus did not give in to Satan's temptation; he responded with the truth: "Thou shalt worship the Lord thy God, and him only shalt thou serve." Third, when dealing with temptation, vow to serve God and God alone. Jesus Christ is our Lord.

God, thank you for making me aware of Satan's tactics so I won't be deceived by his lies. I will not give in to temptation. I will serve you and you alone.

Matthew 4:19
And he saith unto them, Follow me, and I will make you fishers of men.

Jesus said this to Simon Peter and Andrew. They were fishermen by trade; therefore, Jesus was appealing to their nature when he vowed to make them "fishers of men." We too want to be fishers of men; however, the thing to note here is that whatever identity you currently hold—businessman, doctor, student, waitress—God wants to use it for his kingdom. He wants to use your talents and identity to reach people.

Lord, use my identity and skills to reach others. I will follow you in all things.

Matthew 5:2–12

And he opened his mouth, and taught them, saying, Blessed are the poor in spirit: for theirs is the kingdom of heaven. Blessed are they that mourn: for they shall be comforted. Blessed are the meek: for they shall inherit the earth. Blessed are they which do hunger and thirst after righteousness: for they shall be filled. Blessed are the merciful: for they shall obtain mercy. Blessed are the pure in heart: for they shall see God. Blessed are the peacemakers: for they shall be called the children of God. Blessed are they which are persecuted for righteousness' sake: for theirs is the kingdom of heaven. Blessed are ye, when men shall revile you, and persecute you, and shall say all manner of evil against you falsely, for my sake. Rejoice, and be exceeding glad: for great is your reward in heaven: for so persecuted they the prophets which were before you.

The "Sermon on the Mount," as it is called in Matthew, is one of Jesus' premiere pericopes in the Gospels. People gathered on the mountainside to hear Jesus. He sat down, which was the common teaching position of a rabbi. When he opened his mouth, these blessings flowed out.

Blessed are the poor in spirit. Those who are at their wit's end and realize they need God will inherit the kingdom of heaven. Blessed are they that mourn; God will comfort them. Blessed are the meek; those who are humble will inherit the earth. Blessed are those who hunger and thirst for righteousness; they will receive righteousness. Blessed are the merciful; they will obtain mercy. Blessed are those who are pure in heart; the pure will see God. The peacemakers will be called the children of God. Those who are persecuted for his name's sake will be admitted into the kingdom of heaven and will receive a reward. These blessings are promised to those who follow his Word. Let's pray these blessings over our own life.

God, I want to receive all the blessings you have for me. I pray that when I am poor in spirit, when I am mourning and persecuted, you will take care of me. I pray that I will be meek and pure in heart, that I will hunger and thirst after righteousness, and that I will be a peacemaker.

Matthew 5:13–14

Ye are the salt of the earth: but if the salt have lost his savour, wherewith shall it be salted? it is thenceforth good for nothing, but to be cast out, and to be trodden under foot of men. Ye are the light of the world. A city that is set on an hill cannot be hid.

Jesus said we are salt and light. Salt can be used as a preservative; it keeps meat and fish from going bad. Salt also enhances flavor. That's what we ought to be. Without the "salt" of Christ inside of us, the world is bland, meaningless, and rotting.

Light shines in the darkness and overcomes it. Just a little flicker can light up a dark world. So don't hide your light! Let it shine so all can see.

Lord, I want to be salt and light. I want my life to have meaning, and I want to show that meaning to others who are living in darkness.

Matthew 5:21–22

Ye have heard that it was said by them of old time, Thou shalt not kill; and whosoever shall kill shall be in danger of the judgment: but I say unto you, That whosoever is angry with his brother without a cause shall be in danger of the judgment: and whosoever shall say to his brother, Raca, shall be in danger of the council: but whosoever shall say, Thou fool, shall be in danger of hell fire.

Anger can be a deadly thing. This passage shows us it is even more deadly than we thought. Jesus compared anger toward one's brother to killing. (The Complete Jewish Bible reads, "Anyone who nurses anger against his brother will be subject to judgment.") Anger is serious!

Paul said in Ephesians 4:31–32 (NIV), "Get rid of all bitterness, rage and anger, brawling and slander, along with every form of malice. Be kind and compassionate to one another, forgiving each other, just as in Christ God forgave you."

Lord, help me not to be angry with anyone. I want to love as you loved.

Matthew 5:27–28
Ye have heard that it was said by them of old time,
Thou shalt not commit adultery: but I say unto you,
That whosoever looketh on a woman to lust after her
hath committed adultery with her already in his heart.

In this saying, Jesus equated adultery with looking lustfully at a woman. This brings new insight to Paul's admonishment to bring into captivity "every thought to the obedience of Christ" (II Corinthians 10:5). Thoughts can flash through your brain in nano seconds. The key is not to dwell on lustful thoughts. Dismiss them, repent if you need to, and keep on serving God.

Lord, help me not to look on anyone with a lustful spirit. I want to live in the beauty of human relationship the way you designed it.

Matthew 5:38–40

Ye have heard that it hath been said, An eye for an eye, and a tooth for a tooth: but I say unto you, That ye resist not evil: but whosoever shall smite thee on thy right cheek, turn to him the other also. And if any man will sue thee at the law, and take away thy coat, let him have thy cloak also.

Revenge is a terrible thing. Jesus flipped the script on the conventional practice of using the law to get revenge. He said, "We are going to do things differently in my kingdom. We are going to humble ourselves before others."

Lord, help me not to seek revenge when someone hurts me. Rather, I choose not only to forgive but also to give generously to those who hurt me.

Matthew 5:43–45

Ye have heard that it hath been said, Thou shalt love thy neighbour, and hate thine enemy. But I say unto you, Love your enemies, bless them that curse you, do good to them that hate you, and pray for them which despitefully use you, and persecute you; that ye may be the children of your Father which is in heaven: for he maketh his sun to rise on the evil and on the good, and sendeth rain on the just and on the unjust.

Again, Jesus went against the grain of convention by advising his followers to love their enemies. Wow, that's a tough truth to swallow. Think about the person whom you dislike more than any other. They haven't exhibited one ounce of kindness, generosity, or helpfulness. In fact, it seems like their mission in life is to tear you down. Jesus wants you to love that person. Why? Because our God loves everyone. And that person, although misguided, is a person that God wants to see saved. So love them.

Lord, help me to love my enemy as you love all people.

Matthew 5:48
Be ye therefore perfect, even as your Father which is in heaven is perfect.

In Matthew 5, Jesus enumerates commandments that seem to get progressively difficult. The final verse seems to be the hardest of all—be perfect! How could we possibly achieve perfection?

However, the word "perfect" in verse 48 does not mean "completely free from fault or defect." It means "complete, finished, holy," implying we should be sincere and upright in love toward all men. Only God can complete us. Therefore, we do not strive to have zero flaws in our life, but rather to be complete in God. We allow him to empty us so that his attributes can fill us. That is biblical perfection.

Lord, help me to be complete in you.

Matthew 6:3–5

But when thou doest alms, let not thy left hand know what thy right hand doeth: that thine alms may be in secret: and thy Father which seeth in secret himself shall reward thee openly. And when thou prayest, thou shalt not be as the hypocrites are: for they love to pray standing in the synagogues and in the corners of the streets, that they may be seen of men. Verily I say unto you, They have their reward. But thou, when thou prayest, enter into thy closet, and when thou hast shut thy door, pray to thy Father which is in secret; and thy Father which seeth in secret shall reward thee openly.

Jesus taught on giving and prayer. This passage is the prelude to one of the greatest prayers we can pray in Scripture: the Lord's Prayer. However, there is a nugget we can derive from this passage. When we pray and give, we should do it in "secret." We don't boast about our giving or prayer or fasting. We do it as unto the Lord.

Lord, help me to give to you and pray to you in secret. I don't want to be giving and praying just so others can see me; I want to do it in your sight alone. And I know you will reward me openly.

Matthew 6:9–13
After this manner therefore pray ye: Our Father which art in heaven, Hallowed be thy name. Thy kingdom come. Thy will be done in earth, as it is in heaven. Give

us this day our daily bread. And forgive us our debts, as we forgive our debtors. And lead us not into temptation, but deliver us from evil: for thine is the kingdom, and the power, and the glory, for ever. Amen.

This is possibly the greatest prayer we can pray from Scripture. Why? Because this is the model Jesus gave for our prayers. I will discuss this pattern of prayer in greater detail in a later volume, but let's wade into the shallows a little bit.

Prayer should begin by hallowing his name. In this fashion, we start our prayer time with praise and thanksgiving toward the name of God, which is Jesus. We acknowledge his holiness and exalt, worship, bless, and honor his name.

Jesus, your name is great. Your name holds all power in heaven and earth. I praise your name today!

The prayer continues with "Thy kingdom come. Thy will be done in earth, as it is in heaven." There is so much we could take from this verse alone. The key here is that we are praying for the advancement of the kingdom of God on earth. Whatever that is in your life, pray it. If you want to see God's will and kingdom come in your school, pray it. In your family? Pray it. In your church or city? Pray it. We pray that we will follow in his will and be kingdom-minded in all things.

God, I pray that your kingdom would come and your will would be done in every area of my life, as well as in my church, my neighborhood, my school, my place of business, and my community.

"Give us this day our daily bread." Simple enough. We pray for the things we need today. When I pray this prayer, I ask for the strength or bread I need physically, spiritually, emotionally, and mentally.

Lord, I ask for the strength I need physically, spiritually, emotionally, and mentally so I can serve you to the best of my ability throughout this day.

"And forgive us our debts, as we forgive our debtors." We forgive people, and Jesus forgives us. That is the momentum. I like to couple this prayer with one from James 1:19: "Help me to be slow to anger, slow to speak, and quick to forgive."

Lord, I will forgive others who wrong me or owe me something. Help me to be slow to anger, slow to speak, and quick to forgive. And I ask for your forgiveness today, Jesus.

"And lead us not into temptation, but deliver us from evil."

Lord, keep me from temptation, help me to flee from sin, and guard my life from evil.

"For thine is the kingdom, and the power, and the glory, for ever. Amen." We close once again with praise and thanksgiving. We honor God for who he is. And we praise him, for he holds all power.

I praise you, Lord, for you are great. You have all power in heaven and earth. As the psalmist David prayed, "I will extol thee, my God, O king; and I will

bless thy name for ever and ever. . . . I will speak of the glorious honour of thy majesty, and of thy wondrous works." Amen.

Matthew 6:19–21

Lay not up for yourselves treasures upon earth, where moth and rust doth corrupt, and where thieves break through and steal: but lay up for yourselves treasures in heaven, where neither moth nor rust doth corrupt, and where thieves do not break through nor steal: for where your treasure is, there will your heart be also.

Our treasure is in God. What is treasure? It is precious things. For many, time is the most precious commodity they have. For others, it might be their money or their talents and abilities. And for most, it is a combination of all three. We give our time, our talent, and our treasure to God's kingdom.

Lord, I want to invest my treasure in your kingdom by giving you my time and abilities. And I will give to your kingdom financially. Your kingdom is my treasure.

Matthew 6:30–32

Wherefore, if God so clothe the grass of the field, which to day is, and to morrow is cast into the oven, shall he not much more clothe you, O ye of little faith? Therefore take no thought, saying, What shall we eat? or, What shall we drink? or, Wherewithal shall we be clothed? (For after all these things do the Gentiles seek:) for your heavenly Father knoweth that ye have need of all these things.

We, as Christians, don't have to worry about our basic needs: food, clothing, shelter. When we work hard and place our lives in God's hands, we know we will be all right. God created us. He knows what we need and is more than willing to provide for us. So don't worry! Trust in God.

Lord, I will not worry about all the problems in my life. I will trust you, knowing that you are able to provide for me.

Matthew 6:33

But seek ye first the kingdom of God, and his righteousness; and all these things shall be added unto you.

This verse is one of my favorites because of the many promises packed into these twenty words. We seek God first—his kingdom, his treasures, his blessings, his promises, his will, his plan, his desires for our life. We seek his righteousness; we live right, according to his Word. What happens then? All these things shall be added to us! What things? The things from the last prayer we prayed. The things of life. Our worries? Our thoughts about the future? The unknown? God will declare it all if we will seek his kingdom first.

Lord, I want to seek your kingdom first in everything I do. If I succeed in doing that, Jesus, I know you will add all these things—answers to prayers, hope for the future, providential care—unto me.

Matthew 7:1

Judge not, that ye be not judged.

In chapter 7, Jesus said some hard things, beginning with a passage on wrongful judgment. He taught that we should not judge others, especially when we are dealing with sin in our own lives. Some people are too good at finding fault in others while shrugging off their own faults. Jesus called these people hypocrites—which we certainly don't want to be. So take care not to be judgmental. There is a time and place for leaders to address certain situations, but unless we are in a leadership position, it isn't our place to judge.

Lord, help me not to judge others. And let me see the sin in my own life so that I can address it.

Matthew 7:7–11

Ask, and it shall be given you; seek, and ye shall find; knock, and it shall be opened unto you: for every one that asketh receiveth; and he that seeketh findeth; and to him that knocketh it shall be opened. Or what man is there of you, whom if his son ask bread, will he give him a stone? Or if he ask a fish, will he give him a serpent? If ye then, being evil, know how to give good gifts unto your children, how much more shall your Father which is in heaven give good things to them that ask him?

This passage holds great power! Whatever we ask, we can receive. Whatever we seek, we can find. God is a giving God; he is willing to give us our desires. The key is matching up our desires with his plans for us, because he knows what is best for us. When we begin to ask for things that match his desires, our lives become better.

The second portion of this passage describes God as a good gift-giver. Luke 18 tells the story of a persistent widow and a corrupt judge. The widow keeps nagging the judge to rule in her favor until the judge gets fed up and gives in. Thankfully, our God is not a corrupt judge. He is willing and ready to give us blessings. He is a generous giver. Therefore, be persistent. Keep asking! Keep knocking! Don't give up. Know that God has something great in store for you, but you must seek him.

Lord, I will seek after you and all that you have for me. I will ask and knock. And lest I ask amiss, I pray that my desires will be the same desires that you have for my life.

Matthew 7:13–20

Enter ye in at the strait gate: for wide is the gate, and broad is the way, that leadeth to destruction, and many there be which go in thereat: because strait is the gate, and narrow is the way, which leadeth unto life, and few there be that find it. Beware of false prophets, which come to you in sheep's clothing, but inwardly they are ravening wolves. Ye shall know them by their fruits. Do men gather grapes of thorns, or figs of thistles? Even so every good tree bringeth forth good fruit; but a corrupt tree bringeth forth evil fruit. A good tree cannot bring forth evil fruit, neither can a corrupt tree bring forth good fruit. Every tree that bringeth not forth good fruit is hewn down, and cast into the fire. Wherefore by their fruits ye shall know them.

Jesus transitioned his teaching from seeking God to a discussion on eternal life. He proclaimed that the gate and the road that leads to eternal life are narrow, but the road that leads to destruction is broad. We must follow that narrow path. The enemy will set up roadblocks, pitfalls, and place other hindrances in an attempt to make us stumble off the path, but we must stay on it!

While he was on the subject of the narrow path, Jesus began speaking about false prophets. Why? False prophets will throw every weapon in their arsenal at us to get us to veer off the narrow path. How will we know whom to listen to? How will we know who is a true minister and who is evil, deceived, or confused? We will know by identifying the fruit they produce. A true man or woman of God will produce the fruit of the Spirit in their life. They will be connected to the vine, which is Jesus Christ. Look for the fruit of the Spirit and follow after these people on the straight and narrow path.

Lord, I want to follow your path that leads to life. Keep me from those who would try to make me stray

away from the path. And help me to recognize what kind of fruit they are producing so I will know if they are of you.

Matthew 7:24–27

Therefore whosoever heareth these sayings of mine, and doeth them, I will liken him unto a wise man, which built his house upon a rock: and the rain descended, and the floods came, and the winds blew, and beat upon that house; and it fell not: for it was founded upon a rock. And every one that heareth these sayings of mine, and doeth them not, shall be likened unto a foolish man, which built his house upon the sand: and the rain descended, and the floods came, and the winds blew, and beat upon that house; and it fell: and great was the fall of it.

The only safe place to build our house is on the rock, and that rock is Jesus Christ, the chief cornerstone. Everything we do should have Jesus at the foundation. If not, every storm will wipe out our lives like a house built on sand. So we pray that our house will be built on that rock.

Lord, I will build my life with you as the foundation of everything. You are the strength of my life, the rock of my salvation. Everything I say or do will be built upon your name.

Matthew 8:5–10

And when Jesus was entered into Capernaum, there came unto him a centurion, beseeching him, and saying, Lord, my servant lieth at home sick of the palsy, grievously tormented. And Jesus saith unto him, I will come and heal him. The centurion answered and said, Lord, I am not worthy that thou shouldest come under my roof: but speak the word only, and my servant shall be healed. For I am a man under authority, having soldiers under me: and I say to this man, Go, and he goeth; and to another, Come, and he cometh; and to my servant, Do this, and he doeth it. When Jesus heard it, he marvelled, and said to them that followed, Verily I say unto you, I have not found so great faith, no, not in Israel.

There is a prayer embedded in this conversation between Jesus and the centurion. The centurion's servant was very sick, so the commander went and found Jesus. Jesus said he would go to the man's house and heal the servant, but the centurion said, "No, I understand authority, Lord. All you need to do is speak the word and my servant will be healed." Jesus marveled at the man's faith, saying he hadn't found anyone in Israel with that much faith. Anytime Jesus marvels, we should pay attention.

The amazing thing about this story is that later, in Acts 1:8, Jesus proclaimed to the believers that they would receive power. They would have the same authority to speak, and healing would occur. If you have the Spirit of God inside of you through the power of the Holy Ghost, you too have that authority. Speak to diseases. Speak to sicknesses. Speak with authority—not your own authority, but by the authority in the name of Jesus. His name has all authority.

Lord, I will speak with authority to sicknesses and diseases just as you did. I will command people to be healed in Jesus' name.

Matthew 8:23–27

And when he was entered into a ship, his disciples followed him. And, behold, there arose a great tempest in the sea, insomuch that the ship was covered with the waves: but he was asleep. And his disciples came to him, and awoke him, saying, Lord, save us: we perish. And he saith unto them, Why are ye fearful, O ye of little faith? Then he arose, and rebuked the winds and the sea; and there was a great calm. But the men marvelled, saying, What manner of man is this, that even the winds and the sea obey him!

My personal favorite Gospel account of the "Calming of the Storm" is in the book of Mark, and I will expound on the event at that time. But let's deal briefly with Matthew's account. Jesus was sleeping peacefully in the middle of a violent storm. He didn't fear death because he knew his ministry was not yet over and there was more kingdom work to be done.

If God has revealed plans for your life and given you promises, you don't have to fear the storm when it comes. Know that God has a miracle in store for you on the other side of the trial. You may have to go through treacherous waters to get there, but you can trust him to carry out his plan for your life.

Lord, I will not fear my storm. I know you still have work for me to do. Help me to know when it is time to rebuke the storm and when it is time to sleep through it.

Matthew 9:2–8

And, behold, they brought to him a man sick of the palsy, lying on a bed: and Jesus seeing their faith said unto the sick of the palsy; Son, be of good cheer; thy sins be forgiven thee. And, behold, certain of the scribes said within themselves, This man blasphemeth. And Jesus knowing their thoughts said, Wherefore think ye evil in your hearts? For whether is easier, to say, Thy sins be forgiven thee; or to say, Arise, and walk? But that ye may know that the Son of man hath power on earth to forgive sins, (then saith he to the sick of the palsy,) Arise, take up thy bed, and go unto thine house. And he arose, and departed to his house. But when the multitudes saw it, they marvelled, and glorified God, which had given such power unto men.

As a young preacher, I wanted to make an eternal impact. We started having weekly services on the Ball State University campus through Illuminate, our campus ministry. Because of the location and nature of the services, we never knew who was going to show up. Every week, no matter what message God gave me, I would somehow weave in the gospel message—Jesus' death, burial, and resurrection (I Corinthians 15:1–4), which is the similitude of our repentance, baptism, and infilling of the Holy Ghost. The gospel message is the most important thing the world needs to hear.

After a while, I started to wonder, *Why preach about anything else? If the gospel message is the main thing, why preach about miracles, for instance?* The answer came through a combination of real-life experience and biblical study.

First, I had the opportunity to attend overseas crusades with Pastor David Myers and Missionary Charles Robinette. Among other countries, we went to the nation of Bangladesh. This nation was 89 percent Muslim, 10 percent Hindu, and less than 1 percent Christian. People showed up not even knowing why they had come.

That first night in 2019 we had an estimated 7,000 in attendance. We preached about miracles, and three hundred people were healed, including one man who got up out of a wheelchair and walked home. From that moment, we had the attention of the whole city. The mayor even asked the missionary what type of black magic we had brought to his city. James Corbin simply responded, "No magic, just Jesus."

The second night there were over 3,000 claimed miracles, and 380 people raised their hands saying they had spoken in a language they didn't understand. I wondered how that could be when we hadn't even preached about the Holy Ghost. I learned from these elders and mentors in my life that preaching miracles draws people in. Until they see and experience the supernatural, they think you're no different than any other teacher, preacher, or Christian, and they have no reason to believe you.

By the final night of the crusade, the people were ready. They had seen the supernatural; they had experienced miracles. The blind were seeing; the deaf were hearing; tumors were gone. Now it was time to preach the gospel. Our team preached about repentance and the power of the Holy Ghost. That final night, approximately 5,000 people received the gift of the Holy Ghost with the evidence of speaking in other tongues. Two years later, in 2020, we followed the same principle, and the final night there were an estimated 7,000 miracles and 7,000 filled with the Holy Ghost! That's when I realized that miracles draw people in and prove that you have something special. The experience makes them ready to receive the gospel.

Second, Jesus demonstrated this in Matthew 9, when he forgave the palsied man's sins. The scribes in the crowd considered this an act of blasphemy. In their estimation, Jesus, a mere man, was doing something only God could do. Jesus discerned what was in their minds and asked, "Why are you thinking such evil thoughts? Which is easier to say: 'Your sins are forgiven' or 'Stand up and walk'?" The man was still lying there, paralyzed. There was no visible proof that his sins had been forgiven.

Then Jesus said to the paralyzed man, "Arise, take up your bed, and go home." Without any fanfare, the paralytic got up, rolled up his pallet, and walked away. Matthew 9:8 (NKJV) says, "When the multitudes saw it [the miracle], they marveled and glorified God, who had given such power to men." Many people won't listen to you or believe you until they see the supernatural. And the healing of the paralytic was proof that forgiveness of sins had taken place.

I wrote all that to say this: Pray that God will use you to perform and experience miracles. Miracles will bring crowds. Miracles will silence the doubters. Miracles will change lives. Pray for miracles.

Lord, I pray that miracles will come from my ministry. Not for my glory, but so that your name can be glorified. I pray that miracles will open the door for the gospel to be preached and take hold on the hearts and lives of others. In Jesus' name, amen.

Matthew 9:10–12

And it came to pass, as Jesus sat at meat in the house, behold, many publicans and sinners came and sat down with him and his disciples. And when the Pharisees saw it, they said unto his disciples, Why eateth your Master with publicans and sinners? But when Jesus heard that, he said unto them, They that be whole need not a physician, but they that are sick.

Jesus did not associate exclusively with righteous people. Likewise, we should have other people besides Christians in our circle of friends. Friendships are opportunities to spread the light of God. Therefore, it is a tragedy when Christians stay in their own circle and never get out in the world and eat with sinners. We ought to be like Jesus. We ought to have a place, whether it's a club, work, school, a gym—some kind of venue—where we can talk to and reach for others. Pray about this place. And remember that Jesus took his disciples with him. Even Jesus had a guard with him when he was with sinners. If you are being influenced by sinners more than you are influencing them, then you need to rethink your friendships. But if you and a group of church friends can get together and be a light to others, you are acting like Jesus.

Lord, show me the place and the people I can influence in my world. I pray that I would find godly friends to go with me to these venues. I want to be more like you, Jesus.

Matthew 9:20–22

And, behold, a woman, which was diseased with an issue of blood twelve years, came behind him, and touched the hem of his garment: for she said within herself, If I may but touch his garment, I shall be whole. But Jesus turned him about, and when he saw her, he said, Daughter, be of good comfort; thy faith hath made thee whole. And the woman was made whole from that hour.

These three verses show the power of Jesus Christ and the faith that he brought to humanity. This woman was sick for twelve miserable years. Yet she still had hope when she heard about Jesus. I want that kind of persistent faith. Faith that does not give up, no matter how long it takes. Faith that expects something to happen when I touch Jesus.

Lord, I pray for faith like this woman's. I pray that my persistence would continue, no matter how long my problems have been with me. And I pray for the expectation that when I touch you, something good will happen.

Matthew 9:37–38
Then saith he unto his disciples, The harvest truly is plenteous, but the labourers are few; pray ye therefore the Lord of the harvest, that he will send forth labourers into his harvest.

Every time Jesus instructs us on how to pray, we should pay close attention. Here Jesus proclaimed that the harvest would yield a bumper crop. He said, "You don't need to pray for people to be hungry; they are already hungry! They are ready to hear the gospel now!" Unfortunately, Jesus went on to state that the laborers are few. So our prayer should be for laborers. Pray that people will go out and reach others. Pray that people will spread the gospel. Pray that you will be a laborer in the Lord's harvest field.

Lord, I pray for laborers. I pray that you would strengthen those who are already hard at work. I pray for the people you are calling to spread your gospel. Help them to answer the call. And I pray that I would be a laborer for you.

Matthew 10:16
Behold, I send you forth as sheep in the midst of wolves: be ye therefore wise as serpents, and harmless as doves.

Jesus was sending out his twelve disciples to heal and deliver. He knew the enemy would be against them, so he urged the disciples to be "wise as serpents and harmless as doves." To be "harmless" like a dove is to be pure and innocent. Paul gave similar instruction in Romans 10:16 (NIV): "Be wise about what is good, and innocent about what is evil." When we are reaching for others, we should show godly wisdom and purity.

Lord, I pray for wisdom and purity. Help me to demonstrate wisdom and purity when I am spreading your light.

Matthew 10:27
What I tell you in darkness, that speak ye in light: and what ye hear in the ear, that preach ye upon the housetops.

Continuing his instruction on how to reach for others, Jesus told his disciples to speak in public what he had told them in private. Today, Jesus speaks to us through prayer. That's why we must have individual prayer times. Do not expect your ministry for God to be effective if you do not have a private prayer life. Listen for his voice, then speak it to the world.

Lord, I pray that you would speak to me in my private prayer time. Tell me what I should tell others. Show me how I should reach for others. Speak to me, Jesus.

Matthew 11:28–30

Come unto me, all ye that labour and are heavy laden, and I will give you rest. Take my yoke upon you, and learn of me; for I am meek and lowly in heart: and ye shall find rest unto your souls. For my yoke is easy, and my burden is light.

It is at once shameful and comical, but until I was about twenty years old, my image of a "yoke" in the Bible was the yellow center of an egg. But the "yoke" was on me when I found out it had nothing to do with eggs at all. To some of you this may be a revelation. Others of you may be reconsidering the authorship of this book. All jokes aside, the yoke of Jesus Christ is one of our greatest promises.

So what is a yoke? A yoke is a wooden frame that fits over the necks of two oxen, enabling the two animals to work together and share the load. When Jesus spoke of "his yoke," he was talking about our partnership with him. It is interesting because the statements he made seem quite paradoxical. He explained that when we feel as though we are carrying too much weight and burden, we should link up with him because his yoke, or partnership, is "easy" and his burden is "light" for us.

Don't get me wrong. Being yoked with Christ is not effortless; it still requires work. However, the work he gives us is fitting for what we can accomplish with him.

In ancient times, good farmers took care of their hard-working oxen by taking them to the carpenter to order a hand-carved yoke. The carpenter took measurements, then roughed out the yoke. The animals were then brought back, and the carpenter kept adjusting the fit until he was sure the yoke wouldn't chafe while the oxen were working and cause sores.

Another thing a good farmer did was yoke a younger ox with an older, more experienced ox. The older ox would train the younger ox, teaching him proper pacing and how to heed the handler's instructions.

In this passage, Jesus described himself as "meek and lowly in heart." We link up with God because in meekness we find strength. In giving our burdens to God and partnering with him, our burden becomes light. We are yoked together, and the yoke is custom-made for the work he wants us to do. In order for the partnership to work, we must become meek like him. He teaches us go at the right pace, and we meekly heed his instructions.

Lord, I want to partner with you in everything I do. I pray that I would be meek, like you. Take my heavy burdens, Lord, and replace them with your peace and rest.

Matthew 13:16
But blessed are your eyes, for they see: and your ears, for they hear.

We've come to the portion of Matthew where Jesus related many parables to the crowds. Although the subject matter was familiar to the people who heard Jesus' parables, they didn't really comprehend the underlying meaning of what Jesus was saying. At times, the disciples didn't "get it" either, so Jesus explained the meaning of the parables to them privately. In the end, Jesus called his disciples "blessed" because they understood. We should pray for that blessing of understanding.

Lord, open my eyes and ears to see and hear your Word. Open my mind to understand the Scriptures as you did for your disciples. In Jesus' name, amen.

Matthew 14:14
And Jesus went forth, and saw a great multitude, and was moved with compassion toward them, and he healed their sick.

When Jesus was moved with compassion, he performed miracles. That was his way of showing love. Our love for others opens doors to the miraculous. When we act with love and compassion, as Jesus did, miracles can happen. When we look for ways to bless others, God's power will respond.

Compassion unlocks the miraculous. So pray for compassion and pray for miracles.

Lord, I want to be moved by compassion as you were. I pray that miracles would take place as an outgrowth

of my love for others. Let those miracles show people there is a God who loves them.

Matthew 15:30–31

And great multitudes came unto him, having with them those that were lame, blind, dumb, maimed, and many others, and cast them down at Jesus' feet; and he healed them: insomuch that the multitude wondered, when they saw the dumb to speak, the maimed to be whole, the lame to walk, and the blind to see: and they glorified the God of Israel.

Again, we find Jesus healing as an outgrowth of his compassion. Moved with love, he healed all types of diseases and sicknesses. The end of verse 31 records the response of the multitude; they glorified the God of Israel.

Miracles draw crowds. And miracles cause crowds to praise God. That is one of the main reasons God gave us miracles. He not only gives miracles out of his love, but those who witness the miracles end up praising God. I want to see miracles in my city so that others will give praise to God. I want to see miracles everywhere I go so that others will praise him.

God, I pray that miracles will follow my life so that those around me will recognize who you truly are and will give you praise. I pray that your love for people will be shown through the miracles you perform.

Matthew 16:24–26

Then said Jesus unto his disciples, If any man will come after me, let him deny himself, and take up his cross, and follow me. For whosoever will save his life shall lose it: and whosoever will lose his life for my sake shall find it. For what is a man profited, if he shall gain the whole world, and lose his own soul? or what shall a man give in exchange for his soul?

I was recently speaking with a friend on the paradox of Christianity. The granddaddy of all paradoxes in Christianity is the Cross. Jesus died so that we could have life. It was victory in defeat.

We find paradoxes throughout the Bible: Blessed are those who hunger. By taking on his yoke, our burden becomes light. The road that leads to eternal life is difficult. We will receive a crown in heaven, but we will cast it at the feet of Jesus. God is a peaceful warrior. Jesus was fully God, yet fully man. When we are weak, then we are strong.

Christianity is a paradox at its core, and this passage shows us a powerful paradox: "For whosoever will save his life shall lose it: and whosoever will lose his life for my sake shall find it."

Simply put, this means we must give all to him. We *lose* our life to ourselves in order to *gain* and *find* God's life for us. "Losing" our life does not entail physical death; rather, it is the Jesus model of *kenosis*, or self-emptying. We lose our life, identity, dreams, and desires so God can replace them with his plan, his identity for us, his dreams, and his desires for us. The beautiful part about this is that his plans for us are greater than we could imagine. And we are in partnership with him so it is not a drudgery to empty our life; rather, when we empty our life, that is when we truly find it.

God, I empty out my life for your sake. I want you and only you. I want to follow your plan for me. Help me to empty out all my plans so that I can find my life in you.

Matthew 17:21
Howbeit this kind goeth not out
but by prayer and fasting.

This verse comes immediately after the incident when Jesus' disciples could not cast out a devil. After this traumatic failure, they came to Jesus for an explanation. The Master gave them a short talk on faith and concluded, "This kind of power only comes by prayer and fasting."

If there ever was a reason to pray and fast, we find it here. Our praying and fasting produces God-given authority over demons and sicknesses. When we pray and fast, God will move.

Lord, I ask that you will grant authority through my praying and fasting. In Jesus' name, amen.

Matthew 18:1–4

At the same time came the disciples unto Jesus, saying, Who is the greatest in the kingdom of heaven? And Jesus called a little child unto him, and set him in the midst of them, and said, Verily I say unto you, Except ye be converted, and become as little children, ye shall not enter into the kingdom of heaven. Whosoever therefore shall humble himself as this little child, the same is greatest in the kingdom of heaven.

Become like a child—that's how we enter the kingdom of heaven. Children are eager to learn. Ready to act. Easily guided. And best of all, humble, not so much in the sense that their personality is humble, but rather their position in life involves humility. Children are humble because they must depend on adults. Here Jesus is showing us that when we humble ourselves and depend upon him, seek to learn from him, and follow him, we will be able to enter the kingdom of heaven.

Lord, I pray that you would help me to acquire childlike humility. I want to be eager and ready to

learn and respond to your leading. Make me humble so that I will depend upon you for all things. You are my father and I trust you.

Matthew 18:19–20
Again I say unto you, That if two of you shall agree on earth as touching any thing that they shall ask, it shall be done for them of my Father which is in heaven. For where two or three are gathered together in my name, there am I in the midst of them.

We cannot "do" Christianity without others. God designed it that way. He designed the Christian life to be conducted in community. Furthermore, in Matthew 18, we find that all of our praying should not be done in solitude either. While much of our prayer time will be solo, there should be times when we come together with others to pray. When we meet in unity with others, the Lord promised to be "in the midst of them," and whatever is asked in his name "shall be done." That's pretty powerful. So seek friends to pray with. Seek times when you can come together for group prayer.

Lord, I will combine with others in unity of prayer so we can touch heaven and see results. Thank you for your presence in our prayers. In Jesus' name, amen.

Matthew 18:21–22

Then came Peter to him, and said, Lord, how oft shall my brother sin against me, and I forgive him? till seven times? Jesus saith unto him, I say not unto thee, Until seven times: but, Until seventy times seven.

Unforgiveness is like bitter poison. It corrupts, destroys, and erodes your life. In this chapter, Jesus addressed the subject of offense. First, he cautioned us against offending others. Of course, this is often easier said than done, but we try our best not to offend.

Peter wanted to know, "Hey, what about when someone offends me? How many times do I have to forgive them?" Jesus replied 490 times, signifying that we must always forgive—over and over. I often pray in the morning, "Lord, help me to be slow to anger, slow to speak, and quick to forgive." Forgiveness unlocks doors. Forgiveness saves lives.

And forgiveness makes you happy. People who live with unforgiveness can never experience the fullness of joy God has for them. So forgive! Forgive before the offender ever says he or she is sorry. Don't just forgive with your words, but forgive with your actions. Forgive by giving second chances. Forgive by not retaliating. Forgive by walking away from a situation where you were clearly wronged. Forgive by refusing to talk about those who wronged you. Forgive again and again and again. Never stop forgiving. You may learn that you need to stay away from certain people who constantly hurt you, but never stop forgiving. Forgiveness is at the heart of the cross. Forgiveness is at the heart of Jesus.

Lord, help me to forgive others. Even when it's very hard and I've been deeply hurt, help me to forgive. Show me the path I must take toward forgiveness. I pray you will reveal any unforgiveness in my heart. Clean all unforgiveness from my heart, Jesus, so I can forgive others freely.

Matthew 20:26–28

But it shall not be so among you: but whosoever will be great among you, let him be your minister; and whosoever will be chief among you, let him be your servant: even as the Son of man came not to be ministered unto, but to minister, and to give his life a ransom for many.

The greatest calling in the Bible is the calling to minister. This call is to every individual who comes into the kingdom of God. However, few realize what the word "minister" really means. A minister is a servant. As Jesus said, "Whoever will be chief among you, let him be your servant." You see, Jesus' kingdom is an upside-down kingdom, because the leaders are the servers.

Strive to be a minister—a servant—in everything you do. Look to how you can serve your pastor, the elders in your church, your friends, your community, and everyone whom Jesus would serve. That means everybody. Jesus came to be a minister, so, as we become like him, we too should strive to be a minister.

Lord, make me a minister—a servant—like you. Show me how I can serve those around me in my church and my community.

Matthew 21:21–22
Jesus answered and said unto them, Verily I say unto you, If ye have faith, and doubt not, ye shall not only do this which is done to the fig tree, but also if ye shall say unto this mountain, Be thou removed, and be thou cast into the sea; it shall be done. And all things, whatsoever ye shall ask in prayer, believing, ye shall receive.

Jesus brought up the subject of faith throughout the Gospels. Here, he proclaimed that by faith we can speak to mountains and they will be removed, and whatever we ask in prayer, believing, we shall receive. This is powerful! Verse 22 alone provides reason for prayer in our lives. And it again shows us we should pray about everything. Pray and believe, and we will receive.

God, I will pray with faith. I will ask things in your name, bringing everything to you. And I ask that you will increase my faith so my prayers will be powerful.

Matthew 22:14

For many are called, but few are chosen.

This is the second time in Matthew that Jesus has spoken these words. And though we quote them often, I'd like to present a different take on this verse.

Each time Jesus spoke these words, it was in response to believers who either complained or decided not to receive all that was available to them. In Matthew 20, it was to the workers who complained about their wages. In Matthew 22, it was in response to those who were invited, but chose not to attend the wedding.

God calls everyone; it is not his will that any should perish. Salvation is promised to you, to your children, and as many as the Lord shall call. He wants everybody to be saved. In fact, it is his desire that everyone who is called is also chosen. But each individual must decide whether or not they will be chosen. They decide by their actions, their reactions, and their pursuit of the things of God. If they pray and pursue being chosen, then they can be and will be. But few are willing to give their all to him and truly desire to be chosen. Many will be called at youth camps, conventions, conferences, or church services, but few will go home, find a prayer closet every morning, and say, "God, choose me and use me. I'll do whatever it takes if only you will choose me, Lord."

Does God play favorites? It seems like it at the first glance in Scripture. But when you take a deeper look, you will realize that God chooses the ones who are actively pursuing him with everything they have. So go after him! Seek him first! Desire more! Desire to be chosen. Desire the gifts. If you will do this, you will find you are among the few that are chosen.

Lord, I want to be chosen by you. I will pursue you with everything I have. I know you have called me, now I will respond. Use me, Lord.

Matthew 22:36–40

Master, which is the great commandment in the law? Jesus said unto him, Thou shalt love the Lord thy God with all thy heart, and with all thy soul, and with all thy mind. This is the first and great commandment. And the second is like unto it, Thou shalt love thy neighbour as thyself. On these two commandments hang all the law and the prophets.

Jesus made some monumental statements during his three-year ministry on Earth, and this was certainly one of those statements. He summed up all the law and the prophets in two great commandments: love God, and love people. Everything we pray and do should be connected to these two things. If it doesn't show love to God or love to people, then don't take part in it.

The enemy reverses these commandments in his kingdom. The devil's cry to the world is "Hate God, and hate people! Divide them. Cause people to oppose one another on politics, race, wealth, status, nationality, and religion!"

Yes, we in God's kingdom stand up for what is right in the eyes of God, but we do it without attacking the opposition. Jesus stood for what was right without ever attacking the Roman regime. He knew his purpose—to show the love of God by loving people. Let that be our prayer, Lord.

God, I ask that you will help my love for you to deepen. Whether it be through relationship with you or with others, help me to love you more. And help me to show your love to others. I pray that in everything I do or say, let my motivation be to love God and to love people.

Matthew 23:10–12
Neither be ye called masters: for one is your Master, even Christ. But he that is greatest among you shall be your servant. And whosoever shall exalt himself shall be abased; and he that shall humble himself shall be exalted.

Again, we see Jesus speaking of the upside-down nature of his kingdom, where masters are servants and the humble are exalted. It is important to note that this must come from pure motives. We cannot desire humility just so we will be exalted; we must desire to be more like Christ. Only then will we reap the benefits. As long as our motive is to seek him and become like him, we will receive the attendant blessings.

God, I pray that you will humble me. Allow me to be like you—a servant to others.

Matthew 24:3–14

And as he sat upon the mount of Olives, the disciples came unto him privately, saying, Tell us, when shall these things be? and what shall be the sign of thy coming, and of the end of the world? And Jesus answered and said unto them, Take heed that no man deceive you. For many shall come in my name, saying, I am Christ; and shall deceive many. And ye shall hear of wars and rumours of wars: see that ye be not troubled: for all these things must come to pass, but the end is not yet. For nation shall rise against nation, and kingdom against kingdom: and there shall be famines, and pestilences, and earthquakes, in divers places. All these are the beginning of sorrows. Then shall they deliver you up to be afflicted, and shall kill you: and ye shall be hated of all nations for my name's sake. And then shall many be offended, and shall betray one another, and shall hate one another. And many false prophets shall rise, and shall deceive many. And because iniquity shall abound, the love of many shall wax cold. But he that shall endure unto the end, the same shall be saved. And this gospel of the kingdom shall be preached in all the world for a witness unto all nations; and then shall the end come.

Matthew 24 is known as the "end-time chapter." This is a lengthy reading for a prayer, but every line builds upon the last, and in this passage we find many examples of how we should pray in the end time. We are closer to the coming of the Lord than ever before; therefore, we should be praying these prayers.

"Take heed that no man deceive you. For many shall come in my name, saying, I am Christ; and shall deceive many."

Lord, help me not to be deceived by false versions of Christianity. I want my life to be built on the foundation of truth—you are the way, the truth, and the life.

"And ye shall hear of wars and rumours of wars: see that ye be not troubled."

God, help me to stay calm in the midst of the unrest in the world. Reveal your plan to me, Lord. Help me to be a light in the midst of the political and social upheavals around me.

"And then shall many be offended, and shall betray one another, and shall hate one another."

God, I know that in the end time there will be great offense and hate. Please allow me to experience and exhibit trust and love. Help me not to be offended by others, especially in the church. And help me to show your love to everyone.

"And because iniquity shall abound, the love of many shall wax cold."

Lord, remove sin from my life. I don't want anything to stop me from loving you and others.

"But he that shall endure unto the end, the same shall be saved. And this gospel of the kingdom shall be preached in all the world for a witness unto all nations; and then shall the end come."

God, I don't want to just endure; I want to preach your gospel. Help me to proclaim it everywhere I go. You are coming soon; let me keep on proclaiming your truth until you come.

Matthew 25:1–2
Then shall the kingdom of heaven be likened unto ten virgins, which took their lamps, and went forth to meet the bridegroom. And five of them were wise, and five were foolish.

The Parable of the Virgins is the first in a series of parables Jesus gave about the kingdom of God. In this story, ten women had lamps to light their way for the wedding procession. But the bridegroom was delayed, so they all became drowsy and fell asleep. The only difference between these women was that five of them had brought extra oil and five of them had not. A cry arose at midnight, and the foolish five realized their lamps had gone out! They hurried away to purchase more oil. When they returned, it was too late; the bridegroom had already come.

The significance of this passage is that we must be ready at all times for the coming of the Lord. He is merciful, but once he returns to get his bride, the door will be shut. Don't take that chance. Today is the day of salvation!

A backslider who had come back to truth once told me, "There's nothing like laying your head on the pillow at night knowing that if Jesus returns, you are going with him." Be ready!

Lord, I pray that I would be like the five wise virgins in this parable. I want to be ready at all times for your coming, Jesus.

Matthew 25:14–29

For the kingdom of heaven is as a man travelling into a far country, who called his own servants, and delivered unto them his goods. And unto one he gave five talents, to another two, and to another one; to every man according to his several ability; and straightway took his journey. Then he that had received the five talents went and traded with the same, and made them other five talents. And likewise he that had received two, he also gained other two. But he that had received one went and digged in the earth, and hid his lord's money. After a long time the lord of those servants cometh, and reckoneth with them. And so he that had received five talents came and brought other five talents, saying, Lord, thou deliveredst unto me five talents: behold, I have gained beside them five talents more. His lord said unto him, Well done, thou good and faithful servant: thou hast been faithful over a few things, I will make thee ruler over many things: enter thou into the joy of thy lord. He also that had received two talents came and said, Lord, thou deliveredst unto me two talents: behold, I have gained two other talents beside them. His lord said unto him, Well done, good and faithful servant; thou hast been faithful over a few things, I will make thee ruler over many things: enter thou into the joy of thy lord. Then he which had received the one talent came and said, Lord, I knew thee that thou art an hard man, reaping where thou hast not sown, and gathering where thou hast not strawed: and I was afraid, and went and hid thy talent in the earth: lo, there thou hast that is thine. His lord answered and said unto him, Thou wicked and slothful servant, thou knewest that I reap where I sowed not, and gather where I have not strawed: thou oughtest therefore to have put my money to the exchangers, and then at my coming I should have received mine own with usury. Take therefore the talent from him, and give it unto him which hath ten talents. For unto every one that hath shall be given, and he shall have abundance: but from him that hath not shall be taken away even that which he hath.

I'd like to quash the common misconception that the talents the master allotted to his servants were abilities. On the contrary, these talents were bars of either gold or silver. One estimation is that a talent was worth six thousand denarii. Given that one denarius was a single day's wage, one talent was worth what a man would earn in about twenty years. That means Jesus was talking about large sums of money in this parable. Considering they had a six-day work week, the master gave the first man almost a hundred years' worth of wages, the second man almost forty years' worth, and the last man almost twenty years' worth.

This puts the story into a new perspective, because we might tend to feel sorry for the man who received only one talent. *Poor guy. He didn't have much to work with.* I've even heard people compare themselves to the one-talent person in an attempt to show they didn't have much to offer.

I want you to know that the riches of God's kingdom are great, and you have more than you realize. When you calculate the guy with one talent had twenty years' worth of wages, it changes your perspective. Even the "least" in God's kingdom are rich beyond measure!

So don't look down on yourself and your situation any longer. Recognize that God has given much to you. And yes, to whom much is given, much is required. You've got it all—the Spirit, the power, the anointing, the calling, and his kingdom resources. Don't be like the servant who said, "I received only twenty years' worth of wages, so I am just gonna bury the money and sit around in survival mode."

No! If you have this truth, you have more than all the people around you! Recognize your worth! Use it! Invest what you have back into others! Take new territory; multiply the kingdom of God! Make disciples! You can do it!

Lord, I pray that I would recognize my worth in your kingdom. Whether I'm like the guy with five talents or one talent, help me to realize that you've given me so much! Therefore, I will use it to multiply your kingdom in people, territory, and finances. In Jesus' name, amen.

Matthew 26:39–41

And he went a little further, and fell on his face, and prayed, saying, O my Father, if it be possible, let this cup pass from me: nevertheless not as I will, but as thou wilt. And he cometh unto the disciples, and findeth them asleep, and saith unto Peter, What, could ye not watch with me one hour? Watch and pray, that ye enter not into temptation: the spirit indeed is willing, but the flesh is weak.

One of the greatest examples of prayer in the Bible is Jesus praying in the Garden of Gethsemane. He not only prayed with his disciples, but "he went a little further"; he went to a private place in the garden to pray alone. He is our example of a prayer warrior.

When Jesus returned to his disciples, he found them asleep. He said, "Watch and pray, that ye enter not into temptation: the spirit indeed is willing, but the flesh is weak." This is a true statement when it comes to prayer. Our flesh doesn't like to pray; it is our spirit that desires prayer. So go a little further. Keep pushing. Go deeper. Don't fall for the temptation to stop your prayer early. Your spirit is willing.

God, help me to push a little more in my prayer. I pray that I won't give in to my flesh, but rather, I want to be led by your Spirit in prayer.

Matthew 27:54
Now when the centurion, and they that were with him, watching Jesus, saw the earthquake, and those things that were done, they feared greatly, saying, Truly this was the Son of God.

The climax of every Gospel is the Cross. We should always include the Cross in our prayer time. That could be thanking Jesus for the blood he shed and the salvation he obtained for us on the cross, thanking him for the great love he exhibited, praising him for the stripes he endured for our healing, extoling his triumph over evil, and so much more.

In Matthew 27:54, we are introduced to a Roman centurion who previously did not believe in Jesus. But when he witnessed the Cross, he proclaimed, "Truly this was the Son of God!" Our prayer is that when we experience the Cross, we will recognize that Jesus truly is the Son of God. We pray that when others experience the Cross and everything it has to offer, they too will recognize who Jesus is. Let the Cross bring revelation to us and to others.

Jesus, I thank you for the Cross and for all you accomplished on Calvary. I pray that your cross would bring revelation of who you are to me and to others. Help us to recognize you as the almighty God who loves us.

Matthew 28:18–20

And Jesus came and spake unto them, saying, All power is given unto me in heaven and in earth. Go ye therefore, and teach all nations, baptizing them in the name of the Father, and of the Son, and of the Holy Ghost: teaching them to observe all things whatsoever I have commanded you: and, lo, I am with you alway, even unto the end of the world. Amen.

Jesus' final words in Matthew's Gospel are important. He began by proclaiming, "I have all power." So don't worry. Don't fret about your failures. Know that Jesus has all power, and you have him! So go and teach and baptize all nations!

The word *teach* in verse 19 is "make disciples" in the New King James Version. The second usage of *teach* in verse 20 means just that—teach the disciples you have made. This is our commandment, this is our mission, and this is our prayer. Making disciples is not reserved just for the ministry; it is a part of our Christian culture. We don't have an option of whether or not we should make disciples. Making disciples should be our focus. This is what the Cross and the Holy Spirit empowers us to do. So let's go do it!

Lord, help me to make disciples as you commanded in your Word. Train me. Help me to train others. Send me to whatever harvest field you have chosen for me; whether that is my workplace, my school, my community, or another country, I will go.

MARK

Mark 1:3

The voice of one crying in the wilderness, Prepare ye the way of the Lord, make his paths straight.

This opening scene in Mark introduces John the Baptist and tells how the prophet Isaiah foretold that John's ministry was to prepare the way for Jesus Christ (Isaiah 40:3–5). John preceded the first coming of the Lord. His ministry helped line everything up so that when Jesus came, the scene was set.

Jesus is coming back soon. And, like John, we should pray that our ministry will help prepare his way. Like John, we must call people to repentance, and we can also lead them to baptism in the name of Jesus and the infilling of the Holy Spirit. We should pray that we can prepare the way for the Second Coming.

God, help me to be like John the Baptist. I want to prepare the way for your coming. Help me to reach

for others. Help me to make your paths straight, because I know you are coming soon.

Mark 1:12

And immediately the spirit driveth him into the wilderness.

Mark wrote that Jesus was "driven" into the wilderness by the Spirit immediately after his baptism. That verse is worth another read, because there are times where God's Spirit leads us to places we don't necessarily want to go. Moses was led to the wilderness before he ever got to view the Promised Land. Ezekiel was led to a valley of dry bones before he ever saw revival. David was led to take refuge in enemy territory and in desolate caves before he ever moved into the palace. We must allow the Spirit to lead us, because he knows where it is best for us to go.

Lord, I will let your Spirit lead and guide me, even if it means going into a wilderness. I want your plan for my life to be fulfilled.

Mark 1:35

And in the morning, rising up a great while before day, he went out, and departed into a solitary place, and there prayed.

Jesus is our greatest example. In Mark 1:35, we see him rising early in the morning and finding a place to pray alone. His life teaches us this principle: get up early, find a spot, and pray. Seek after God. Seek his will for your life. Pray for others. And pray for strength for that day.

Why did Jesus get up early? Well, he had a busy day of ministry and healing ahead of him. Jesus wanted that personal alone time in prayer before his day began. If you pray for your day at the end of the day, you've already missed it. But praying for your day at the beginning puts your day in line with the will of God for that day. If you can't get up early, pray first. Let prayer be the first words out of your lips in the morning. Seek his counsel first.

God, I will rise up early, find a place alone, and pray, just as you did.

Mark 3:5

And when he had looked round about on them with anger, being grieved for the hardness of their hearts, he saith unto the man, Stretch forth thine hand. And he stretched it out: and his hand was restored whole as the other.

The Gospel writers recorded many miracles performed by Jesus. In this account, a man with a withered hand happened to be in the synagogue when Jesus came in. The Pharisees were aware of the man's presence and of his deformity, and they were watching Jesus like hawks. After discussing with the Pharisees whether it was lawful to heal on the Sabbath, Jesus said to the impaired man, "Stretch forth thine hand."

This is significant because (1) the man's hand was useless, (2) he was incapable of obeying the command, but (3) he had to perform the action before he received his healing. Using all his effort, the man stretched forth his hand, and it was instantly restored.

When seeking a healing or an answer, you may be required to stretch your faith. You may have to step out of your comfort zone. You may have to attempt something it seems impossible for you to do before Jesus will answer. But as soon as you take that small step of faith toward God, he will meet you, speak with you, and heal you.

God, help me to stretch my faith whether it's for a healing or an answer to prayer. Help me to stretch my faith with the expectation that you will provide.

Mark 3:27

No man can enter into a strong man's house, and spoil his goods, except he will first bind the strong man; and then he will spoil his house.

One of my greatest passions as a college student—and still is today—was campus ministry. I remember my good friend Mike McGurk speaking on this passage at an Awakening Campus Ministry Conference. He pointed out that the enemy has been on our campuses a lot longer than we have. We have power and authority through the Holy Ghost, but we need to exercise it; we need to bind the strong man. We left that CMI conference and began to pray over our campus. We met in the mornings, we did prayer walks at night, we prayed in different locations, and we prayed as we entered and left the campus. One semester we recognized we had authority because about fifteen students were filled with the Holy Ghost on the Ball State University campus.

If there is a university or college campus in your city, be aware that it's the seat of the enemy, especially if it is a long-term institution. There may have been up to a hundred years of sinful activity going on there. But it is not the strong man's territory; it is God's territory.

When you walk into new territory, the enemy doesn't want you to take it. You must bind the strong man and declare the authority you possess by the power of the Holy Ghost. Whether it is your school, your workplace, your community center, your gym, or whatever harvest field you are working in, bind the enemy, loose peace, and claim new territory for the kingdom of God.

I will bind the strong man in my harvest field. I will take new territory for the kingdom of God. In Jesus' name, amen.

Mark 4:14–20

The sower soweth the word. And these are they by the way side, where the word is sown; but when they have heard, Satan cometh immediately, and taketh away the word that was sown in their hearts. And these are they likewise which are sown on stony ground; who, when they have heard the word, immediately receive it with gladness; and have no root in themselves, and so endure but for a time: afterward, when affliction or persecution ariseth for the word's sake, immediately they are offended. And these are they which are sown among thorns; such as hear the word, and the cares of this world, and the deceitfulness of riches, and the lusts of other things entering in, choke the word, and it becometh unfruitful. And these are they which are sown on good ground; such as hear the word, and receive it, and bring forth fruit, some thirtyfold, some sixty, and some an hundred.

Jesus used this parable to show his disciples that when they preached the gospel, results would vary according to the situation and response of the people who heard the word. Some have suggested this parable means we will retain only 20 percent of the harvest. However, it is not God's will that anybody should perish; we all have a choice to come to salvation.

I think this parable shows us our prayer and responsibility to sow the seed of God's Word to everyone and pray that it will fall on good ground. But ultimately, our job is just to sow the Word. As Paul said, "Some plant, some water, but God gives the increase."

Lord, I will sow your Word in all situations and to all people. I pray that when your Word lands on the hearts and minds of people that it will take root. I pray that others would allow your Word to grow in their life.

Mark 4:30–32

And he said, Whereunto shall we liken the kingdom of God? or with what comparison shall we compare it? It is like a grain of mustard seed, which, when it is sown in the earth, is less than all the seeds that be in the earth: but when it is sown, it groweth up, and becometh greater than all herbs, and shooteth out great branches; so that the fowls of the air may lodge under the shadow of it.

This mustard-seed analogy was recorded by Matthew, Mark, and Luke. Jesus used this parable to teach people the nature of the kingdom of God.

Although mustard seeds are tiny, the plant can grow up to twenty feet tall. Each yellow flower develops into an elongated pod containing four to eight seeds. A mustard plant can yield 350 to 7,900 seeds, depending on the variety of mustard.

Jesus explained that sowing seed into God's kingdom has exponential return. When you store your "treasures" in heaven, God rains down multiplied blessings. You have to plant and water the seed, but when you do, the yield is far greater than you could ever imagine!

God, I will sow seed in your kingdom. And I pray that your kingdom will produce a multiplication of growth in my life.

Mark 4:37–39
And there arose a great storm of wind, and the waves beat into the ship, so that it was now full.
And he [Jesus] was in the hinder part of the ship, asleep on a pillow: and they awake him, and say unto him, Master, carest thou not that we perish?
And he arose, and rebuked the wind, and said unto the sea, Peace, be still. And the wind ceased, and there was a great calm.

These three verses in Mark paint one of my favorite pictures of the New Testament. Jesus was teaching a great crowd somewhere along the western shore of the Sea of Galilee. He taught while sitting in a boat, and his voice carried over the water to the multitude on the shore. When he finished telling the Parable of the Mustard Seed, Jesus told his disciples he wanted to go across the lake.

The Sea of Galilee is known for sudden violent storms. The cooler air masses swoop down from the surrounding mountains and collide with the warmer air in the lake's basin, producing sudden, fierce storms. Waves can measure up to ten feet high. Many of the disciples were fishermen by trade, and they knew enough to be afraid of these storms.

Exhausted from his day of teaching, Jesus lay down in the back of the boat and went to sleep. The possibility of a sudden squall didn't worry him because he is always in control.

The storm hit, and billows were threatening to swamp not only the disciples' boat, but other little ships that were bobbing crazily on the waves. It wasn't looking good. Frantic, the disciples woke Jesus and asked, "Master, don't you care that we're about to die here?" Jesus got up from his nap, rebuked the wind, spoke to the sea, and everything was peaceful again.

My favorite part of this amazing story is what Jesus said to the wind: "Peace, be still." The Greek word for "be still" in Mark 4:39 is *phimoo,* meaning to "bind the mouth with a muzzle or to make speechless." He essentially told the wind to shut its mouth. It is the same word with which Jesus silenced the demon in Mark 1:25 and Luke 4:35. He told the enemy to shut up.

We can take this one step further. The devil is known as the "prince of the power of the air" in Ephesians 2:2. His voice is the wind in our storm. He lies to us that the waves are too strong, that we can't handle it, and that we are going to die. In reality, the wind is what causes the waves. That's why the first thing Jesus did was rebuke the wind.

You must rebuke that liar that speaks to you and tell him to shut up. Muzzle his mouth so he can't speak to you in your storm. You have the authority. Rebuke the thoughts he puts into your head. Speak to the prince of the power of the air and muzzle him in Jesus' name.

Devil, I rebuke your lies right now in my life. I command you to be still. I'm placing a muzzle on your lying mouth, and I will receive the calm and peace of God in the middle of my storm.

Mark 5:22–23

And, behold, there cometh one of the rulers of the synagogue, Jairus by name; and when he saw him, he fell at his feet, and besought him greatly, saying, My little daughter lieth at the point of death: I pray thee, come and lay thy hands on her, that she may be healed; and she shall live.

Jairus had position and power as a ruler of a synagogue. But he knew what to do when his daughter lay dying; Jairus came to Jesus, fell at his feet, and prayed. Prayer is symbolic of petition—asking God for something. Jairus said, "I pray thee, come and lay thy hands on her, that she may be healed; and she shall live." First, this ruler of the synagogue knew where to go, and second, he knew what to say. He asked Jesus to heal his daughter, believing that if the Lord would come, she would live. Have faith in your prayer!

Jesus, I come to you with my need. I fall down at your feet, asking you to heal so that _____ may live.

Mark 5:28
For she said, If I may touch but his clothes,
I shall be whole.

Jesus had every intention of going with Jairus, despite the crowd that thronged him. But their journey was interrupted by the woman with the issue of blood. For twelve years this woman had gone to every available physician and spent all her money without getting any better. Then she heard about Jesus. She didn't sigh and say, "I'll just try this one last time, and if that doesn't work it's all over." No, with her faith soaring she said, "If I can just touch his robe, I shall be healed!" I love when the Bible uses that word "shall." It is definite. It will happen. Believe that when you go to God, no matter what else you've tried, it will happen.

God, give me big faith. Give me faith to speak that it shall happen when I come to you.

Mark 5:36

As soon as Jesus heard the word that was spoken, he saith unto the ruler of the synagogue, Be not afraid, only believe.

After the woman was healed from her ailment and sent on her way in peace, a messenger came to Jairus and said, "Don't trouble the Master any further. Your daughter has died." This did not intimidate Jesus. He simply said to Jairus, "Don't be afraid; only believe."

They came to the house of Jairus, and Jesus entered the room where the daughter lay dead. If it had been us walking into that room and seeing the dead girl, we may have thought, *If only the crowd hadn't been pressing all around me, I could have arrived sooner. If only I hadn't let that sick woman cause further delay, we might have got here in time to see this girl healed. If only . . .*

Jairus, the one who at first had approached Jesus with great faith, began to doubt. Because even when you declare healing, it sometimes doesn't work out the way you think it will. As soon as the news came that his daughter had died, Jairus faced doubt again.

Jesus simply answered him, "Be not afraid, only believe." What God says is final! Even when your story, your prayer, or your request takes an unexpected turn, believe!

Lord, I will trust what you have spoken when my situation takes a bad turn. I will return to my faith that I had in the beginning, believing you will finish what you started.

Mark 6:31
And he said unto them, Come ye yourselves apart
into a desert place, and rest a while:
for there were many coming and going,
and they had no leisure so much as to eat.

Jesus believed in rest so much that he said to his disciples, "Let's go off by ourselves to a quiet place and rest awhile" (NLT). They boarded a boat and headed off to a place where they thought no one would bother them.

In our culture, rest is hard to come by. The essence of ministry means you are constantly surrounded by others. Beyond that, your phone makes you accessible 24/7. It is difficult for a minister to find a time or a place to rest. But that is why we, like Jesus and his disciples, have to create the time and place to rest. We must be intentional about it. At times, we may need to depart to a quiet place. We may need to set everything aside and take time to relax. Rest is not carnal; it is spiritual.

It also is important to note that Jesus and his disciples didn't wait until all the needs had been met before they found a place to rest. Why? Because needs will always be there. But Jesus knew that rest was more important to the future than the present needs in front of them. So we pray that God would direct us in seasons of rest.

Lord, help me to know when it is time to rest. Lead me to a quiet place when I need to rest, even if I don't want to or I don't feel like it's a good time. Teach me how to rest as you did.

Mark 6:46

And when he had sent them away,
he departed into a mountain to pray.

Their rest was short-lived. Jesus was recognized, and people poured out of the cities in droves, anticipating where the disciples were headed. When Jesus and the disciples landed on the beach, there was a crowd of about five thousand people waiting for them. Jesus taught them the rest of the day, and toward evening the people were hungry, so Jesus fed them all with five loaves and two fish. Then he sent the people away so he could pray.

We must recognize that our foundation is not ministry. Serving others is our calling; it is the design for our lives as Christians. But the foundation of our relationship with God is prayer.

Lord, help me to build a relationship with you through prayer and to found my ministry on prayer. Help me to balance the two. I will seek you first.

Mark 8:23–25

And he took the blind man by the hand, and led him out of the town; and when he had spit on his eyes, and put his hands upon him, he asked him if he saw ought. And he looked up, and said, I see men as trees, walking. After that he put his hands again upon his eyes, and made him look up: and he was restored, and saw every man clearly.

An Old Testament example of praying more than once would be Elijah praying for rain until he saw a cloud the size of a man's hand. In this New Testament passage, Jesus prayed for a man, but he was only partially healed. The man could see, but his vision was blurred. So what did Jesus do? He prayed again, and "put his hands again upon his eyes." Don't get discouraged if your first prayer doesn't seem to work. Continue to have faith and pray again.

After Jesus touched the man's eyes, Jesus told him to "look up." Looking up is an action that expresses the expectation to receive something. When Peter and John were at the gate called Beautiful, the lame man looked up. Jesus encouraged this blind man to perform an act of faith.

Whether you are praying for yourself or for others, don't become discouraged. Keep on praying, look up, and be fully restored.

Lord, I will continue to pray when there is only gradual healing. I will expect full restoration by faith.

Mark 8:34

And when he had called the people unto him with his disciples also, he said unto them, Whosoever will come after me, let him deny himself, and take up his cross, and follow me.

What does it mean to deny yourself, take up your cross, and follow Jesus? It could mean a variety of things for different people. However, the key is that following Jesus costs you something.

I recently had a conversation with Kris and Ken Dillingham. Their definition of a disciple is someone who is serious enough about following God that they will allow him to change what they care about. Following Jesus will change you. Your desires will become his desires. The more time you spend with him, the more you will learn to deny yourself, take up your cross, and follow him. Your motives will become his motives, and his plan will supersede the plan you had for your life. And as you deny yourself, your flesh, and your own plan, he will take care of you.

Every Christian has a cross. It may be the sin of your past—the pain, the guilt, the shame, the hurt. It may be your history and what's been done to you. When you pick up your cross, it is heavy. However, you don't have to bear your burden alone; you can lay it at the feet of Jesus. In this way, you deny yourself. You deny your pride to be independent and carry everything yourself. You accept your brokenness. As the next verse states, you lose your life in order to find it through Christ. You follow Jesus.

God, I will deny myself, take up my cross, and follow you. I will lay everything at your feet. Teach me your ways, Master. You are my Lord, my teacher, and my Savior.

Mark 9:29

And he said unto them, This kind can come forth by nothing, but by prayer and fasting.

We need to recognize the fact that we have authority through the name of Jesus. God has given us this authority in the same way he gave it to his disciples. However, we must submit to that authority and exercise that authority. How? By prayer and fasting.

God, lead me to a life marked by much prayer and fasting. Take me deeper and closer to you through prayer and fasting. Teach me how to use authority through prayer and fasting. In Jesus' name, amen.

Mark 9:35

And he sat down, and called the twelve, and saith unto them, If any man desire to be first, the same shall be last of all, and servant of all.

In first-century Greco-Roman culture, humility meant something like "crushed" or "debased." It was associated with failure and shame. Thus, Jesus was not admired for being humble. The Greco-Roman world was not impressed that Jesus was "meek and lowly."

Jesus was the prototype for servant leadership. Today, many businesses practice this model of servant leadership, but it was Jesus who first paved the way. His kingdom is an upside-down kingdom (i.e., the last shall be first and the first shall be last; the humblest servant shall be the greatest leader). Jesus modeled this throughout the Gospels.

So aim to serve others of all statuses. The more you serve, the more you will become like Jesus.

Lord, help me to serve in your kingdom. Show me whom to serve, when to serve, and how to serve. Not for accolades or so that I can gain status in your kingdom, but rather to spread your love and be more like you.

Mark 9:42–43

And whosoever shall offend one of these little ones that believe in me, it is better for him that a millstone were hanged about his neck, and he were cast into the sea. And if thy hand offend thee, cut it off:

it is better for thee to enter into life maimed,
than having two hands to go into hell,
into the fire that never shall be quenched.

Offense is a deadly weapon of the enemy. It will destroy others and destroy you. Jesus spoke hyperbolically on the topic of spiritual offense. While he didn't mean someone will place a literal millstone around your neck if you cause spiritual harm to a believer, or that you should cut off your hand if you commit sin, Jesus was sending a message to avoid offense. Try not to offend others, and keep away from sin.

Lord, I pray against offense in my life. I do not want to offend others, and I do not want to commit sin. Give me clarity of thought. Lead me in your paths.

Mark 10:7–9
For this cause shall a man leave his father and mother, and cleave to his wife; and they twain shall be one flesh: so then they are no more twain, but one

flesh. What therefore God hath joined together, let not man put asunder.

God designed marriage. And as the New Living Translation states, "Since they are no longer two but one, let no one split apart what God has joined together." We pray against anything that would come between marriage partners, whether that is your own marriage, your parents' marriage, your pastor's marriage, or others you know. Pray for strong marriages. Pray for unity.

Lord, I pray for marriages in this world, but especially in the church, because strong families make strong churches. I rebuke every attack of the enemy on marriages. Marriage is God's design, and no weapon formed against it shall prosper.

Mark 10:29–31
And Jesus answered and said, Verily I say unto you, There is no man that hath left house, or brethren, or sisters, or father, or mother, or wife, or children, or lands, for my sake, and the gospel's, but he

shall receive an hundredfold now in this time, houses, and brethren, and sisters, and mothers, and children, and lands, with persecutions; and in the world to come eternal life. But many that are first shall be last; and the last first.

As we've discussed earlier, following after Jesus costs us something. However, in this passage Jesus stated that those who have given up something or someone for the kingdom's sake will receive "an hundredfold" not only in the world to come, but during their lifetime on Earth. Walk in the blessings God has for you! Realize the eternal blessings of the Lord and keep on pursuing him.

God, help me to recognize the blessings you are giving me both in this life and in the world to come. I will constantly pursue you.

Mark 10:43–45
But so shall it not be among you: but whosoever will be great among you, shall be your minister: and whosoever of you will be the chiefest, shall be servant

of all. For even the Son of man came not to be ministered unto, but to minister, and to give his life a ransom for many.

I want to be like Jesus. His ultimate mission was to serve and give his life for others. While I will never die on a cross for others, I can give myself to others in service. In this kingdom, the greatest carry a towel and a basin. The greatest are those who serve others and are constantly looking to lift others up. Become a servant.

Jesus, I want to be a servant like you. Help me to give of my time, talent, and treasure to others so they may be lifted up.

Mark 11:22–26

And Jesus answering saith unto them, Have faith in God. For verily I say unto you, That whosoever shall say unto this mountain, Be thou removed, and be thou cast into the sea; and shall not doubt in his heart, but shall believe that those things which he saith shall come to pass; he shall have whatsoever he saith.

Therefore I say unto you, What things soever ye desire, when ye pray, believe that ye receive them, and ye shall have them. And when ye stand praying, forgive, if ye have ought against any: that your Father also which is in heaven may forgive you your trespasses. But if ye do not forgive, neither will your Father which is in heaven forgive your trespasses.

It is interesting that Jesus coupled faith and forgiveness in the same passage. Forgiveness unlocks faith; unforgiveness is a faith-blocker. You cannot access belief until you believe the Word of God. And his Word is full of forgiveness and mercy. Choose forgiveness and then have faith. Have faith that anything can happen!

Lord, rid me of any unforgiveness. Increase my faith, and help me not to harbor doubt in my heart. Help me to pray big prayers.

Mark 12:17

And Jesus answering said unto them, Render to Caesar the things that are Caesar's, and to God the things that are God's. And they marvelled at him.

Knowing that God is in charge of the big picture, we sometimes spiritualize things that are not really spiritual and forget that we live in a world that is largely run by the unchurched. In Mark 12:17, we learn that the things that belong to this world are simply a fact of life. It is our responsibility to give to God what belongs to God and not worry about the things that belong to the world.

Lord, help me to understand what is yours. I don't want to worry about the things of this world. I will give to the world what belongs to the world and give to you what belongs to you.

Mark 12:29–31

And Jesus answered him, The first of all the commandments is, Hear, O Israel; The Lord our God is one Lord: and thou shalt love the Lord thy God with all thy heart, and with all thy soul, and with all thy mind, and with all thy strength: this is the first commandment. And the second is like, namely this, Thou shalt love thy neighbour as thyself. There is none other commandment greater than these.

Our God is one, and we should love him with everything we have. He loves people, which means we should too. We should love other people as much as we love ourselves. It is that simple.

Lord, I will love you and love people in everything I do. You are the one true God.

Mark 12:41–44
And Jesus sat over against the treasury, and beheld how the people cast money into the treasury: and many that were rich cast in much. And there came a certain poor widow, and she threw in two mites, which make a farthing. And he called unto him his disciples, and saith unto them, Verily I say unto you, That this poor widow hath cast more in, than all they which have cast into the treasury: for all they did cast

in of their abundance; but she of her want did cast in all that she had, even all her living.

There is a time to go all in. This widow gave all she had, which wasn't much. *Holman's Bible Dictionary* says she dropped two of the smallest copper coins available into the treasury. They were worth only a fraction of a penny. Yet Jesus said her contribution was greater than any of the others.

This widow didn't receive a temporal blessing that we know of. She did not receive any public accolades. In fact, we don't know anything else about her. But privately, Jesus said this woman was amazing. Go all in.

Like the widow woman, I want to go all in, God. Not just in my finances, but in my efforts in living for you. And although my contribution may be small in comparison to others, I want to give you all I have and all I am.

Mark 13:32–33

But of that day and that hour knoweth no man, no, not the angels which are in heaven, neither the Son, but the Father. Take ye heed, watch and pray: for ye know not when the time is.

Mark 13 gives a little insight into the return of Jesus Christ. There will be wars and deception and betrayal and desolation. The gospel will be preached among all nations. Then Jesus revealed, "But of that day and that hour knoweth no man." Why would he tell us the signs of his coming but then say nobody knows exactly when it will happen? He was giving us fair warning to look for the signs and make sure we are keeping our relationship with him current. If ever we should have a prayer life, it is now. He is coming soon, so watch and pray.

Lord, I will watch for the signs of your coming, and I will pray. I will pray for understanding, for strength, for direction, and for counsel. I will pray that your gospel will be preached in all nations. And I will act on my prayers.

Mark 14:38

Watch ye and pray, lest ye enter into temptation. The spirit truly is ready, but the flesh is weak.

Whenever we see Jesus praying or teaching on prayer, we should take heed. In this scene, Jesus was praying in the Garden of Gethsemane. The disciples were so weary that they kept falling asleep. Jesus told them their spirit was ready and willing to pray, but their flesh was weak.

Push through! Keep on going! Even when you don't feel like it, keep pushing through in prayer. Eventually you will get past your flesh and into the next dimension in prayer. The spirit is willing, so keep on praying.

Jesus, help me to keep on pushing in prayer even when I don't feel like it. Help me not to give in to the temptation to quit. I am willing to go further.

Mark 15:37–39

And Jesus cried with a loud voice, and gave up the ghost. And the veil of the temple was rent in twain from the top to the bottom. And when the centurion, which stood over against him, saw that he so cried out, and gave up the ghost, he said, Truly this man was the Son of God.

The tearing of the veil symbolizes that access to an intimate relationship with God is no longer exclusive. Whosoever will can enter into relationship with him. So proclaim the gospel! Proclaim that Jesus is the Son of God—God manifest in the flesh! And the promise of salvation is available to all.

Jesus, thank you for the relationship you made available to all mankind through your death on the cross. Thank you for forgiveness and for the blood you shed.

Mark 16:15–18

And he said unto them, Go ye into all the world, and preach the gospel to every creature. He that believeth and is baptized shall be saved; but he that believeth not shall be damned. And these signs shall follow them that believe; In my name shall they cast out devils; they shall speak with new tongues; they shall take up serpents; and if they drink any deadly thing, it shall not hurt them; they shall lay hands on the sick, and they shall recover.

The Bible says that these signs *shall* follow them that believe. You are a believer, so exercise your faith! Expect miracles!

Lord, as a believer, I pray that these signs shall follow me: I will have authority, speak in tongues, lay hands on the sick, and glory in your protection against harm and danger. In Jesus' name!

LUKE

Luke 1:30

And the angel said unto her, Fear not, Mary: for thou hast found favour with God.

When we think of Bible characters who had favor with God, our mind often goes to this passage. However, I think Mary's favor is often overlooked as some supernatural one-off experience. The truth is Mary *found* favor. How? Through her actions. She was devoted. She was committed. She was extraordinary. She did what others neglected to do. And for that reason, she was favored and chosen.

It seems there is a difference between grace and favor; grace is given, but favor is "found." For example, many translations render Genesis 6:8, "Noah found favor in the eyes of the LORD." The NET note on Genesis 6:8 says, "'Find favor' is a Hebrew idiom meaning 'to be an object of another's favorable disposition or action; to be a recipient of another's favor, kindness, mercy. The favor/kindness is often earned, coming in response to an action or condition." Favor is not just being called, but also being chosen. Favor gives a mark of distinction. And it is God's design that all his children walk in favor—favor that produces blessings and opportunities, both spiritual and temporal. More important, favor that produces relationship.

God, I want to find favor with you, and I will do whatever I have to do to enter into a deeper relationship with you. I want to be extraordinary. Show me how to find favor.

Luke 2:52

And Jesus increased in wisdom and stature, and in favour with God and man.

We should be growing in these four areas: wisdom, stature, favor with God, and favor with man. Growing in wisdom is simply learning. We should aim to learn. Learn from others, from prayer, from the Word of God, from books, and from experience. Every situation is a learning opportunity.

Growing in stature is growing in maturity. This mainly comes with time and experience. Don't neglect or rue or deny the ups and downs of life. You are growing, and it is a slow, sometimes painful process that lasts a lifetime.

We talked about favor with God in the last prayer, but Jesus also grew in favor with man. Getting closer to God should not exclude you from people. Yes, growing deeper in relationship with God does require solitude, but remember who Jesus was—a man of the people. His purpose was to take us in deeper relationship with God, and he accomplished that in his own life by seeking and developing relationships with others. So grow in favor with people. Learn how to treat people kindly. Show yourself friendly. Work on learning these four things. Pray for growth in your life.

Lord, I pray that I would grow in wisdom, stature, and in favor with God and man.

Luke 3:4–6
As it is written in the book of the words of Esaias the prophet, saying, The voice of one crying in the

wilderness, Prepare ye the way of the Lord, make his paths straight. Every valley shall be filled, and every mountain and hill shall be brought low; and the crooked shall be made straight, and the rough ways shall be made smooth; and all flesh shall see the salvation of God.

Not long ago the Lord began to deal with me on this passage. Shortly before Jesus came the first time, God called a man to prepare the way of the Lord. The prophet Isaiah likened this man to a voice crying in the wilderness, prophesying that all flesh would see the salvation of God. Before the Lord returns again, the world needs to hear a voice crying out that they can "see the salvation of God"!

I don't believe there is just one or two, but many who will be that voice. I want to be that voice. I want you to be that voice. If you are called by God, you should want to be that voice too.

Jesus, give me the strength and boldness to stand and proclaim your soon coming. Allow me to prepare the

way for your return. And I pray that all flesh shall see the salvation of God.

Luke 4:1

And Jesus being full of the Holy Ghost returned from Jordan, and was led by the Spirit into the wilderness.

This takes a few reads to truly comprehend what the Scripture is implying here. It doesn't seem right that the Spirit would lead Jesus into the wilderness—to his temptation. The wilderness was neither good nor pleasant, but it served a vital purpose. Jesus faced the enemy in the wilderness; he was tested and tried. He proved himself and came out on top. When Jesus left the wilderness, he left with authority. After the wilderness, Jesus proclaimed that the Spirit had come upon him. In the next prayer, we will pray about what happens after the wilderness. But Luke 4:1 is a difficult prayer to pray because we may have to submit to a wilderness experience.

Lord, let your Spirit lead me wherever you need to take me. If you lead me to a wilderness, I will go.

Luke 4:18–19

The Spirit of the Lord is upon me, because he hath anointed me to preach the gospel to the poor; he hath sent me to heal the brokenhearted, to preach deliverance to the captives, and recovering of sight to the blind, to set at liberty them that are bruised, to preach the acceptable year of the Lord.

After Jesus came out of the wilderness, he proclaimed his mission. If it was his mission, we should want it to be our mission. What is the mission? *People* are the mission. Jesus said the Spirit had anointed him to preach the gospel to the poor. "To preach" means to proclaim. So speak it! Pray that you will find the poor and proclaim the gospel. You would be shocked who around you is needy. News flash: it's everyone! But God will give an inheritance to those who believe and obey the gospel. So find those who need him and proclaim the gospel!

Next, he said to heal the brokenhearted, preach deliverance to the captives, recover sight to the blind, and set at liberty them that are bruised. Jesus is here for hurting people. Again, you never know who is hurting around you, so aim to heal. The Spirit has anointed you to preach deliverance. Pray for the blind. I have seen physically blind people healed and spiritually blind people healed. I have received direction myself in a moment of blindness. Preach liberty, freedom, and peace to those who are bruised, broken, and defeated. Show them Jesus. You can't give them anything, but you can preach Jesus.

Finally, Jesus said he was anointed to preach the acceptable year of the Lord. This entire passage is a quote from the prophet Isaiah, and Jesus fulfilled Isaiah's prophecy. Similarly, we continue to preach the acceptable year. We continue to proclaim his rule, his reign, and his soon coming.

Lord, I want to act on your mission. Help me to help others. Anoint me to preach the gospel to the needy, to heal the brokenhearted, to preach deliverance to the captives, recovering of sight to the blind, and to preach the acceptable year of the Lord.

Luke 4:32

And they were astonished at his doctrine:

for his word was with power.

Jesus taught with authority and power. The Greek word for doctrine refers to teaching, or what is being taught. The people were astonished at Jesus' powerful teaching. He did not teach against the law; but rather, he taught to fulfill it. We should seek not only to be anointed, but also to be filled with doctrine by diligently studying his Word.

God, I will study your Word and pray that you will fill my mind and heart with correct doctrine. And let your doctrine that I speak come forth with power.

Luke 4:43

And he said unto them, I must preach the kingdom of God to other cities also: for therefore am I sent.

You should not cease to preach when you leave your own city. In reality, when you are led by the Spirit, everywhere you go is a missions trip!

I recently took a vacation to Peru. People asked me if I was on a missions trip, and I mistakenly said no. It turned out that every person we talked to was hungry for God, as if God was placing the hungry in our path. I'll share one specific story here.

As I was boarding a flight from Lima to Cusco, there was an open seat next to mine. I thought it was going to stay empty for the entire flight, but then a girl entered the plane wearing a New York Yankees hat. As she walked down the aisle, I was trying to figure out if she spoke Spanish or English. If it was Spanish, I would attempt to get through a conversation, but my Spanish was pretty rusty. She came down the aisle, took the seat next to me, flashed a Canadian passport, and then asked me, "Hey, do you know how long this flight is?" English! We were good to go.

We started talking, and I asked what she did. She said, "I'm an indigenous faith healer." She asked the same of me and I responded, "I'm a preacher." She started laughing at the coincidence of an indigenous faith healer and a preacher sitting next to each other on a plane. It seemed like the first line of a bad joke.

We started to share different stories of healings and spiritual encounters. I used her language as we talked. She knew very little about the Bible, but I could tell she was hungry and searching. Yet she was confident in who she was. She explained that all things had a spirit—trees, people, even her water bottle. I talked about *the Spirit* and how the spiritual energy she would feel in one of our church services would be pretty strong. But she replied, "I'm comfortable with where I am."

To be honest, I wasn't sure if I missed it. Maybe she wasn't hungry. But in reality, she had been conditioned to believe a certain thing about Christianity, and that's all she knew. She proceeded to talk about spirits, then she said, "And, of course, in everything there is always the unknown."

I had an *aha* moment. Maybe it was the Spirit of the Lord that came upon me. Maybe it was a spiritual gift or the Holy Ghost prompting. More than anything, it was simply living a life ready to proclaim the gospel at any point in any city. I got out my Bible and opened to Acts 17, where Paul was talking to the Athenians at Mars' Hill. He told them they were too "superstitious" (fearful of the gods), as if their altar "To the Unknown God" had been erected lest they offended a god they weren't aware of. Paul proceeded to tell them this unknown God's name was Jesus. He preached to them in their language, with their words, so they could understand. I preached Paul's sermon to the girl, and we spent the rest of the flight studying the Word of God.

We turned to passages from the Old Testament through the New Testament. We talked about the revelation of the name of Jesus. I shared with her that every healing that took place happened in the name of the "known" God. The God that she called the "Source," I called Jesus. I showed her the plan of salvation and how that plan gave the people power. And she was soaking it up.

When we had finished our Jesus Bible study, she looked at me and said, "Wow. So what do I need to do?" My mouth almost dropped open. She was asking the same question they had asked in Acts 2:37 right before Peter revealed the plan of salvation. I immediately flipped back to Acts 2:38 and said, "This is it right here! This is what you need to do!" She said,

"Can I take a picture of that?" I said, "Sure! You can also write it down. It is Acts 2:38."

When I said those words, she got excited and said, "2:38?! Are you kidding me? Riley, I've been seeing the number 2:38 since I was sixteen years old. Everywhere I look I see 2:38. It's my spiritual number!" I told her, "This is a God thing, and Jesus is calling you."

This is one incredible story, but it's more than a story. It is a prayer. We should desire encounters like this. Before this moment ever happened, I had heard stories from Josh Herring and Charles Robinette of how God used them to witness on planes. I want God to use me to preach his gospel to other people in other cities.

You too can see this happen. Be ready! Be ready to proclaim the gospel not just in your church, not just in your city, but everywhere you go. You never know when, where, or how God will use you!

Lord, use me to preach your gospel everywhere I go. I must preach the gospel in other cities. Lead me to the hungry, Jesus. And give me an opportunity to speak about you.

Luke 5:16
And he withdrew himself
into the wilderness, and prayed.

Luke 5:15 (NLT) says, "The report of his power spread even faster, and vast crowds came to hear him preach and to be healed of their diseases." Jesus was constantly surrounded by throngs of needy people. The only way he could get any rest and a chance to recharge was to withdraw into a quiet place and find a spot alone to pray.

Do not mistake ministry for relationship. Being constantly about the Master's business will not deepen your relationship with him. You have to find a place and time to work on your relationship with God. In fact, it seems that the more *ministry* you are doing, the more you need that alone time to spend growing your relationship with him.

Lord, in the middle of helping others, allow me to find a time and a place to be alone with you.

Luke 6:12

And it came to pass in those days, that he went out into a mountain to pray, and continued all night in prayer to God.

Jesus had all-night prayer meetings. At the end of this particular prayer meeting, he chose his disciples. That's pretty powerful. If you want to take prayer to a new level, I encourage you to try an all-night prayer meeting. Plan it out. Set times and topics of prayer. It will seem hard at first, but it will take you to a deeper relationship with God.

Lord, call me to an all-night prayer meeting. I want to draw closer to you.

Luke 6:27–28

But I say unto you which hear, Love your enemies, do good to them which hate you, Bless them that curse you, and pray for them which despitefully use you.

The Bible says the world will know we are disciples of Jesus by the way we love one another. In this passage,

Jesus explained this doesn't just refer to the people we like. Everybody loves their family and friends. But as Christians, we must love those who hate us.

This hard saying gives new perspective to our motives. We must always remember that we are not against people. Whether those people are in government, in business, in war, or in healthcare doesn't matter; we are not against people. We may be against the spirit that is on people, but we are commanded to love people and pray for people. It is never right to curse people and pray for their downfall, because no matter how badly they have acted, their actions were instigated by the spirit behind those actions. So pray against the spirit, but pray for your enemies.

God, I pray for my enemies because they need you just as much as I do. I pray against the spirit that motivated them to take unfortunate actions, and I pray that you would help them find their way to you.

Luke 6:37–38

Judge not, and ye shall not be judged: condemn not, and ye shall not be condemned: forgive, and ye shall be forgiven: give, and it shall be given unto you; good measure, pressed down, and shaken together, and running over, shall men give into your bosom. For with the same measure that ye mete withal it shall be measured to you again.

We don't judge others; we forgive others. Judgment is God's job. Our job is simply to love people. Furthermore, it is our privilege to give to God and his kingdom. Many times, that means giving to others. And when we give, it is given back to us pressed down, shaken together, and running over.

One of the best analogies I've heard regarding this verse is a trash can. The trash can is full, but you've got something more to throw away, so you press the contents down to make room for the extra trash.

The psalmist said, "Blessed be the Lord, who daily loadeth us with benefits, even the God of our salvation" (Psalm 68:19). Jesus is constantly adding benefits to our lives, but sometimes he wants to put in something extra, so he presses everything down to make room for more. What a great and generous Savior!

Lord, I won't judge; rather, I will forgive and give. And I pray you will give back to me pressed down, shaken together, and running over.

Luke 6:45
A good man out of the good treasure of his heart bringeth forth that which is good; and an evil man out of the evil treasure of his heart bringeth forth that which is evil: for of the abundance of the heart his mouth speaketh.

What we say matters, so speak life. Speak promises. Speak good treasures. Talk about good things. Because what you say reflects what is in your heart.

Lord, I will speak good things throughout my day.

Luke 8:5–8

A sower went out to sow his seed: and as he sowed, some fell by the way side; and it was trodden down, and the fowls of the air devoured it. And some fell upon a rock; and as soon as it was sprung up, it withered away, because it lacked moisture. And some fell among thorns; and the thorns sprang up with it, and choked it. And other fell on good ground, and sprang up, and bare fruit an hundredfold. And when he had said these things, he cried, He that hath ears to hear, let him hear.

The Parable of the Sower certainly plays out in our efforts to spread the gospel. Sometimes it appears that every time we tell someone about Jesus the seed is stomped out by the devil, or it fails to take root, or it is choked by the pleasures/cares of life. But never fear; some of that precious seed will land on good ground, so that is what we pray for—good ground.

Lord, I pray that when I spread your gospel it will fall on good ground. Lead me to people who are hungry to receive the seed of the Word.

Luke 9:1–2

Then he called his twelve disciples together, and gave them power and authority over all devils, and to cure diseases. And he sent them to preach the kingdom of God, and to heal the sick.

Just as Jesus gave power and authority to his disciples to preach the kingdom of God and heal the sick, he has given that same authority to you. If you have the Holy Ghost, you possess that power. Believe it! Know it! And use it!

Lord, help me to recognize the power, the authority, and the call you have given to me. Give me boldness to exercise that authority that others might be saved and healed.

Luke 9:23–24

And he said to them all, If any man will come after me, let him deny himself, and take up his cross daily, and follow me. For whosoever will save his life shall lose it: but whosoever will lose his life for my sake, the same shall save it.

It is not easy to "buy in" to the lifestyle of following Jesus, because the cost is steep—it costs us everything. But once we "lose our life," we actually end up saving it because Jesus becomes our provider, our healer, our deliverer, our Savior, and our friend. He is our everything. He is our life.

Jesus, I will deny myself. I will deny my pride to figure everything out myself. I will take up my cross and follow you. I will lose my life so that you can save it. You are so good!

Luke 9:49–50
And John answered and said, Master, we saw one casting out devils in thy name; and we forbad him, because he followeth not with us.
And Jesus said unto him, Forbid him not:
for he that is not against us is for us.

In this short passage, Jesus answered a question we are still dealing with today. John came and said, "Hey, Jesus, we saw some people casting out demons in your name, but they aren't obeying everything you teach. They aren't in our group, and they don't have the full truth. What should we do about these people?" Jesus responded, "Don't stop them. If they are not against us, they are for us."

Sometimes it seems as if Christianity has more denominations and opinions than there are stars in the heavens. A lot of preferences have become doctrines, and a lot of truths have been neglected. But this passage indicates that as long as these people are using his name and they're not against us, they are for us.

However, notice that Jesus did not say, "That's okay. Let's just join them and all come together in unity." There are some Christians who believe we should all get together and become one big group. While Jesus did not forbid churches without the whole truth to continue casting out devils in his name, he did not allow his disciples to settle for less. He had called his disciples to truth, and he expected them to live out his commandments.

In our prayer, we must recognize there are Christians around us who don't follow Jesus in the same manner we do. In fact, there are Christians who have misguided beliefs and practices. We are not exempt from ever getting a faulty idea; we all fall short at times. But we should be striving daily to seek after truth and obey truth. And while we're doing that, we should not forbid those who are proclaiming Jesus.

Jesus, help me to navigate through those who proclaim your name but don't completely follow after you, your teachings, and your commandments. I will not forbid those people, but neither will I forsake the truth you have given me.

Luke 10:2

Therefore said he unto them, The harvest truly is great, but the labourers are few: pray ye therefore the Lord of the harvest, that he would send forth labourers into his harvest.

Surface observations of the people around you may lead you to believe no one is truly hungry for God, but believe it; there are hungry people everywhere! Jesus said the harvest is great, but rather than praying for the harvest, Jesus said pray that people would go and reach the hungry. First, we should want to be a laborer. Second, we should pray for both current and future laborers.

Lord, I want to be a laborer. And I pray for all the laborers out there now—missionaries, preachers, pastors, saints, evangelists, Bible study teachers, and all those who are sowing the seed of the Word. I pray that those you have called will step up and join the ranks of laborers in your harvest.

Luke 10:27

And he answering said, Thou shalt love the Lord thy God with all thy heart, and with all thy soul, and with all thy strength, and with all thy mind; and thy neighbour as thyself.

This is our constant prayer: "Lord, I will love you with all my heart, soul, strength, and mind. And I will love my neighbor as myself." However, it is more than just a prayer we pray. Our prayers must become actions. We must follow through on our prayers.

God, I will love you with all my heart, soul, strength, and mind. And I will love others as myself.

Luke 10:39–42

And she had a sister called Mary, which also sat at Jesus' feet, and heard his word. But Martha was cumbered about much serving, and came to him, and said, Lord, dost thou not care that my sister hath left me to serve alone? bid her therefore that she help me. And Jesus answered and said unto her, Martha, Martha, thou art careful and troubled about many things: but one thing is needful: and Mary hath chosen that good part, which shall not be taken away from her.

Martha was serving, which is a good thing. However, there are times when serving is not the most important thing. Jesus said Mary had chosen the "good part"; she was sitting at Jesus' feet.

Don't get so caught up in ministry that you forget to spend time with the God you are serving. The object of our worship—Jesus Christ—is the most important thing. As one preacher said, "We are called to love God before we are called to love others." Of course, our ministry is based on serving others, but our time with others should not overtake our time worshiping God.

Lord, I will worship you in all things. I won't get so caught up in serving that I forget to spend time worshiping you.

Luke 11:1–4

And it came to pass, that, as he was praying in a certain place, when he ceased, one of his disciples said unto him, Lord, teach us to pray, as John also taught his disciples. And he said unto them, When ye pray, say, Our Father which art in heaven, Hallowed be thy name. Thy kingdom come. Thy will be done, as in heaven, so in earth. Give us day by day our daily bread. And forgive us our sins; for we also forgive every one that is indebted to us. And lead us not into temptation; but deliver us from evil.

This model prayer explains the premise of this book: "Teach us to pray." There will be a more in-depth analysis of The Lord's Prayer in book five about daily prayers and relationship prayers; however, let's highlight a few things in Luke's account of the Lord teaching his disciples to pray.

Jesus began with, "Our Father which art in heaven, Hallowed be thy name." He began with praise and worship.

Lord, I praise your holy, glorious name!

He continued, "Thy kingdom come. Thy will be done, as in heaven, so in earth." After spending some time praising the name of Jesus, we pray kingdom prayers.

Lord, let your kingdom come. I pray that your will would be done in every area of my life. I pray that you would rule and reign on this earth as you do in heaven.

"Give us day by day our daily bread. And forgive us our sins; for we also forgive every one that is indebted to us." Here we pray for our physical and spiritual needs for today and for forgiveness.

Lord, I pray for every need I have today. And I pray that you would forgive me as I forgive others.

"And lead us not into temptation; but deliver us from evil."

God, keep me from temptation today. Deliver me and protect me from the evil one.

Luke 11:9–10
And I say unto you, Ask, and it shall be given you; seek, and ye shall find; knock, and it shall be opened unto you. For every one that asketh receiveth; and he that seeketh findeth; and to him that knocketh it shall be opened.

Jesus is telling us to seek and knock. This is not to say we will receive everything we want, but we can expect to receive the things that are spiritually beneficial.

Jesus wants to see our true desire, our desperation. And when we pursue him, he will answer.

Jesus, I will keep on seeking. I will keep on knocking. I will keep on asking until I receive an answer from you.

Luke 12:12
For the Holy Ghost shall teach you in the same hour what ye ought to say.

In the church's infancy, disciples were arrested and put on trial before magistrates and Jewish leaders for acting on their faith in Jesus Christ. While many areas of the world today do not arrest Christians for preaching or witnessing in Jesus' name, the world still judges. We are still "put on trial" in our everyday conversation. We may not face the death penalty, but we must still be ready to give an answer. The Bible says that in times like these the Holy Ghost will teach us what we need to say. That is our prayer.

Lord, I pray that your Holy Spirit that dwells in me will teach me what to say when people ask me questions about my faith in you. I will study, but I also need your Spirit to guide my answers.

Luke 12:27–32

Consider the lilies how they grow: they toil not, they spin not; and yet I say unto you, that Solomon in all his glory was not arrayed like one of these. If then God so clothe the grass, which is to day in the field, and to morrow is cast into the oven; how much more will he clothe you, O ye of little faith? And seek not ye what ye shall eat, or what ye shall drink, neither be ye of doubtful mind. For all these things do the nations of the world seek after: and your Father knoweth that ye have need of these things. But rather seek ye the kingdom of God; and all these things shall be added unto you. Fear not, little flock; for it is your Father's good pleasure to give you the kingdom.

Think about it. The Creator provides for life forms all around you. If he protects and provides for the flowers of the field, how much more will he protect and provide for you? Don't worry about what comes next in your life. Trust in the fact that God will make a way. Just keep on seeking his kingdom. Keep on walking by faith. For it is his good pleasure to give you the kingdom.

Lord, increase my trust in you as I continue to walk by faith and seek your kingdom. I will trust that you take pleasure in granting me entrance into your kingdom. I praise you for your faithfulness and goodness! I delight in your Word.

Luke 12:37

Blessed are those servants, whom the lord when he cometh shall find watching: verily I say unto you, that he shall gird himself, and make them to sit down to meat, and will come forth and serve them.

Don't get so caught up in the busyness of life that you forget Jesus is coming soon. Watching for his coming doesn't mean staring out your window, waiting for the sky to split open. It means to keep on seeking his kingdom. Keep praying. Keep fasting. Keep listening.

Keep reaching for others. Doing all of these things is the essence of watching for his coming.

Lord, I want to be ready when you come. Help me to be faithful and obedient and actively "watching" for your return.

Luke 13:18–19

Then said he, Unto what is the kingdom of God like? and whereunto shall I resemble it? It is like a grain of mustard seed, which a man took, and cast into his garden; and it grew, and waxed a great tree; and the fowls of the air lodged in the branches of it.

We often say that we should have faith like a grain of mustard seed to show that we only need a little bit of faith. But that does not address this entire passage. Jesus said his kingdom is like a grain of mustard seed that *grows*. The mustard seed is the smallest seed, but it grows over time. In similar fashion, our faith may start out small, but it should keep growing.

Lord, let my faith grow exponentially like a grain of mustard seed.

Luke 15:4–7

What man of you, having an hundred sheep, if he lose one of them, doth not leave the ninety and nine in the wilderness, and go after that which is lost, until he find it? And when he hath found it, he layeth it on his shoulders, rejoicing. And when he cometh home, he calleth together his friends and neighbours, saying unto them, Rejoice with me; for I have found my sheep which was lost. I say unto you, that likewise joy shall be in heaven over one sinner that repenteth, more than over ninety and nine just persons, which need no repentance.

Luke 15 contains three stories about lost things: the lost sheep, the lost coin, and the lost prodigal son. In each of these stories, the main character rejoices over something he/she has lost. In the story of the lost sheep, the main character is the shepherd.

Jesus is the good shepherd, and he rejoices over every lost person who comes into his fold.

Furthermore, the Bible says that heaven rejoices over one sinner who repents more than it rejoices over those who "need no repentance." We must understand that *everyone* needs repentance, so the people who "need no repentance" are those who, like the Pharisees, think they are so righteous they don't need to repent.

In this passage, we want to model our prayer to be like Jesus. Like Jesus, we should rejoice over every lost person that repents. Every time they repent, we should keep on rejoicing!

Lord, I will rejoice when the lost return home.

Luke 16:13
No servant can serve two masters: for either he will hate the one, and love the other; or else he will hold to the one, and despise the other. Ye cannot serve God and mammon.

Mammon means money. If you are constantly worrying about money, you are serving money.

Instead, you should work hard and let God take care of your money. Put it in his capable hands.

Lord, I give my finances to you. I chose to serve you rather than money.

Luke 17:1
Then said he unto the disciples, It is impossible but that offences will come: but woe unto him, through whom they come!

Jesus introduced an important topic in Luke 17:1: the danger of causing others to stumble. "Although the temptation to commit this sin is ever present, one must at any cost avoid using his influence to lead astray a seemingly insignificant, vulnerable disciple or perhaps would-be follower of Christ ('one of these little ones') from the faith" (Apostolic Study Bible).

Jesus underlined the seriousness of causing this kind of offense in verse 2: "It were better for him that a millstone were hanged about his neck, and he cast into the sea, than that he should offend one of these little ones."

Rather, we should seek to edify others. To edify someone is to encourage their spiritual growth and character development, to instruct or improve. Paul was keen on people edifying one another. In Ephesians 4:12, he said the fivefold ministry was given for the edification of the saints. In Romans 14:19, he urged following after the things "which make for peace, and things wherewith one may edify another." In Romans 15:2–3, he wrote, "Let every one of us please his neighbour for his good to edification. For even Christ pleased not himself." In I Thessalonians 5:11, he wrote, "Wherefore comfort yourselves together, and edify one another."

Lord, keep me from causing the kind of offense you warned against in Luke 17:1. Help me not to harm someone else, even unintentionally. Instead, help me to be an encourager and an edifier. I want to help others to make it to heaven.

Luke 18:1–8

And he spake a parable unto them to this end, that men ought always to pray, and not to faint; saying,

There was in a city a judge, which feared not God, neither regarded man: and there was a widow in that city; and she came unto him, saying, Avenge me of mine adversary. And he would not for a while: but afterward he said within himself, Though I fear not God, nor regard man; yet because this widow troubleth me, I will avenge her, lest by her continual coming she weary me. And the Lord said, Hear what the unjust judge saith. And shall not God avenge his own elect, which cry day and night unto him, though he bear long with them? I tell you that he will avenge them speedily. Nevertheless when the Son of man cometh, shall he find faith on the earth?

In the Parable of the Importunate Widow, the widow comes before the unjust judge and asks him to rule in her favor. The judge ignores her. The widow keeps coming back so many times that the judge finally gets fed up and gives her what she wants.

Jesus then flipped the script by saying if this unjust judge would help the poor widow, how much more will our God help us! Our God is just. And as we consistently talk to him, he answers us speedily.

God, I will continue to ask things of you. I will pray without ceasing. I know you are good and just and will answer speedily.

Luke 18:10–14
Two men went up into the temple to pray; the one a Pharisee, and the other a publican. The Pharisee stood and prayed thus with himself, God, I thank thee, that I am not as other men are, extortioners, unjust, adulterers, or even as this publican. I fast twice in the week, I give tithes of all that I possess.
And the publican, standing afar off, would not lift up so much as his eyes unto heaven, but smote upon his breast, saying, God be merciful to me a sinner. I tell you, this man went down to his house justified rather than the other: for every one that exalteth himself shall be abased; and he that humbleth himself shall be exalted.

God is not impressed with our boasting. We don't need to tell him how good we are or brag about all the great things we have done. Only God is perfect. And as the age-old quote goes, "We don't need to get good to get God. We get God to get good." Don't try to impress God; rather, humble yourself. Humility is always the correct approach before God.

Lord, I will not boast or try to impress you. I will approach you with humility.

Luke 19:46
Saying unto them, It is written, My house is the house of prayer: but ye have made it a den of thieves.

Even Jesus got upset and acted in righteous anger when he entered the outer court of the temple and found professional moneychangers and animal vendors plying their trade.

Jews came to Jerusalem from all over the world to worship, bringing with them the money of their country, which was unacceptable in Jerusalem, and especially in the temple. The moneychangers knew the value of foreign monies, and some of them took advantage by lending money and charging as much as three hundred percent interest per year *(Holman Bible Dictionary).*

The foreign Jews exchanged their money for temple coins to purchase animals or birds for sacrifices. You can imagine the chaos and noise generated by the crowds milling about, the clinking of coins, the arguments between lenders and borrowers, the shouting of animals handlers, the lowing of oxen, bleating of sheep, and cooing of doves. It was a chaotic mess!

No wonder Jesus was upset and drove them out! These people were corrupting the true purpose of the temple. They had transformed the pure worship of God into a money-making scheme. Jesus declared, "My house is a house of prayer!"

Lord, I will reverence your house and make it a house of prayer. I will behave myself wisely and humbly in your presence.

Luke 20:38
For he is not a God of the dead,
but of the living: for all live unto him.

This passage gives us two reasons to praise God. First, our God is alive, and he hears our every prayer. Second, Jesus is showing us the promise of eternal life. He stated in the previous verse that God is the God of Abraham, Isaac, and Jacob. These patriarchs will one day be resurrected. Therefore, we praise God for eternal life.

Jesus, I praise you because you are alive! And you will one day give us eternal life, as you promised.

Luke 21:8–11

And he said, Take heed that ye be not deceived: for many shall come in my name, saying, I am Christ; and the time draweth near: go ye not therefore after them. But when ye shall hear of wars and commotions, be not terrified: for these things must first come to pass; but the end is not by and by. Then said he unto them, Nation shall rise against nation, and kingdom against kingdom:
and great earthquakes shall be in divers places,

and famines, and pestilences; and fearful sights and
great signs shall there be from heaven.

Luke 21 is the parallel of Matthew 24. We pray the same prayer here that we prayed in Matthew 24, that we won't be deceived or afraid.

The closer we get to the end time the scarier world conditions are going to be. There will be wars and diseases and earthquakes and fearful sights in the heavens. We need to keep our eyes focused on the prize. Don't be deceived. Keep trusting God's truth.

Lord, I pray that I will not be deceived or afraid as the time of the Second Coming draws nearer. Help me to keep my eyes on you.

Luke 21:28
And when these things begin to come to pass,
then look up, and lift up your heads;
for your redemption draweth nigh.

What exactly should we do when the world gets crazy? What should we do right now? The Bible says to look up because our redemption draweth nigh. Redemption is the action of gaining possession of something in exchange for payment. Jesus paid the price and will redeem us in our trouble. Just keep holding on. Look up and stay ready because Jesus is coming soon!

God, when the world gets crazy, I choose to look toward you. Our redemption is coming soon.

Luke 22:19–20

And he took bread, and gave thanks, and brake it, and gave unto them, saying, This is my body which is given for you: this do in remembrance of me. Likewise also the cup after supper, saying, This cup is the new testament in my blood, which is shed for you.

This communion ceremony shows us how we ought to remember the Cross. When we partake of the communion service, we don't just do it mechanically; we do it thankfully and prayerfully. We think about Jesus and praise him for what he did on Calvary.

John wrote, "He is the propitiation for our sins: and not for ours only, but also for the sins of the whole world" (I John 2:2). Paul wrote, "Whom God hath set forth to be a propitiation through faith in his blood, to declare his righteousness for the remission of sins that are past, through the forbearance of God" (Romans 3:25).

The Greek word for *propitiation* means "atoning sacrifice; an appeasement to satisfy an angry, offended party." Christ's atoning blood appeased God's wrath against the sins of the world. Jesus willingly laid down his life on Calvary and bore the brunt of God's wrath that we might receive remission of sins. Therefore, we glorify and honor him for the pain and shame he bore, the flogging he endured, and the blood he shed. We remember his atoning death on the cross.

Jesus, I will remember your cross. You are the mighty God, and I thank and praise you for the blood you shed for me.

Luke 22:26

But ye shall not be so: but he that is greatest among you, let him be as the younger; and he that is chief, as he that doth serve.

In the poignant atmosphere during the Last Supper, as Jesus once again explained his purpose and imminent death, he reiterated this principle: serve others. Serving others is the heartbeat of God.

Lord, I promise to serve others in every way that I can.

Luke 22:31–32

And the Lord said, Simon, Simon, behold, Satan hath desired to have you, that he may sift you as wheat: but I have prayed for thee, that thy faith fail not: and when thou art converted, strengthen thy brethren.

There are many interesting points we could pull from this passage, but I'd like to home in on the fact that Jesus prayed for others. The main focus of this book has been about the personal prayers we should pray over our lives according to Scripture. However, we should never neglect to pray for others. Jesus said that Satan had desired Simon Peter. Both Jesus and the enemy knew that Peter would be a powerful minister. So Jesus prayed for Peter.

The more time you spend in ministry the more you realize that the enemy attacks those who are powerful. Whether through family, finances, health, or mind, the enemy is constantly working against the ministry. So pray for your ministry friends and leaders. Pray that their faith would not fail and that God would strengthen them.

God, I pray for ministers right now. I pray for my friends who are doing a work for you. I pray that you would strengthen them and that their faith would not fail.

Luke 22:42

Saying, Father, if thou be willing, remove this cup from me: nevertheless not my will, but thine, be done.

Jesus was not at all thrilled about the task he had to accomplish. In his humanity, he "agonized over His approaching death and the effect of God's wrath" (Nelson Study Bible). He cried out, "Father, if it is Your will, take this cup away from Me" (NKJV). Nevertheless, he submitted to God's will.

There are times when God's plan for our life is not panning out the way we thought it would. He always has our end goal in mind, but the process can get pretty rough. In those times we too must pray, "Nevertheless, not my will, but thine be done."

Jesus, when your will for my life doesn't seem pleasant, I will still submit to you. I want your will to be accomplished in my life, Lord.

Luke 23:34

Then said Jesus, Father, forgive them;
for they know not what they do.
And they parted his raiment, and cast lots.

There is no greater story of forgiveness than the life of Jesus. As God manifested in flesh, he demonstrated his love for others by healing them, teaching them, feeding them, having compassion on them, crying over them, and praying for them. Then the very people he had come to minister to demanded that he be crucified, the cruelest form of execution by the Roman government. Jesus then prayed that his executioners would be forgiven, because they didn't understand the significance and repercussions of their actions.

Even when people are nasty and hateful and act like they would rather see you dead than alive, still pray that God would forgive them. We hate sin, but we love people and want to see them saved. So pray that God will forgive and reach for those who have wronged you. (See Luke 6:28.)

Lord, I pray that you would forgive those who have wronged me.

Luke 23:45–46

And the sun was darkened, and the veil of the temple was rent in the midst. And when Jesus had cried with a loud voice, he said, Father, into thy hands I commend my spirit: and having said thus, he gave up the ghost.

Jesus' physical act of death changed the world forever, bringing spiritual and physical manifestations with it. In the physical world, the veil was torn in two. Why was this significant?

This linen veil was a thick, heavy, elaborately embroidered hanging that separated the Holy Place from the Most Holy Place. Only the high priest had access to the Most Holy Place, and that only once a year. On the Day of Atonement, he would push aside the heavy veil and encounter the glittering Ark of the Covenant hovered over by golden angels. He would move over to the Ark with a bowlful of sacrificial blood and sprinkle it on the Mercy Seat.

When Jesus died, this thick veil was torn in two from top to bottom, an act that could only have been done by the hand of God. Spiritually, the tearing of the veil changed the relationship between God and mankind. No longer was access to his holy presence limited to an exclusive few at an appointed time. Now, all are accepted by God through the atoning death of Jesus Christ. We don't need a priest to intercede on our behalf; we can approach God ourselves anywhere, anytime. The writer of Hebrews proclaimed, "Let us therefore come boldly unto the throne of grace, that we may obtain mercy, and find grace to help in the time of need" (Hebrews 4:16).

Jesus, thank you for offering yourself as a sacrifice on the cross and for tearing the veil at the time of your death on Calvary. Thank you that I now have the opportunity to come into your presence and worship you anytime, anywhere.

Luke 24:47–49

And that repentance and remission of sins should be preached in his name among all nations, beginning at Jerusalem. And ye are witnesses of these things. And, behold, I send the promise of my Father upon you: but tarry ye in the city of Jerusalem, until ye be endued with power from on high.

Jesus' final words in Luke were that his followers should preach repentance and remission of sins, and that they should go to Jerusalem and pray until they received power from on high.

In Acts 1, also written by Luke, we see this power is the Holy Ghost, evidenced by speaking in other tongues. If you have not received this power, follow the words of Jesus. Pray to receive it! Because if you pray for it, you will receive it.

Lord, I will tell the good news of repentance and remission of sins everywhere I go. And I pray that you will fill me with the Holy Ghost and power. I want that power living down inside of me to be a witness for you.

JOHN

John 1:5

And the light shineth in darkness;
and the darkness comprehended it not.

Jesus was the Word in the beginning. He is the one and only God. The Bible says that he, the Light, shined in the darkness, but the darkness "comprehended it not." Other translations say the darkness "couldn't overcome" the light, "didn't' understand" the light, and "can never extinguish" the light. His light is all powerful! And we pray that his light inside of us will reflect outward to others.

God, you are the light of the world. I pray that I will be a reflection of your light. When others look at me, let them see your light shining through me.

John 1:40–42

One of the two which heard John speak, and followed him, was Andrew, Simon Peter's brother. He first

findeth his own brother Simon, and saith unto him,
We have found the Messias, which is, being
interpreted, the Christ. And he brought him to Jesus.
And when Jesus beheld him, he said, Thou art Simon
the son of Jona: thou shalt be called Cephas,
which is by interpretation, A stone.

When Andrew first met Jesus, he ran to get his brother and exclaimed, "Hey, Simon! We have found the Christ! We have found the Savior!" Andrew's first reaction was to tell someone else the good news. When he introduced Simon to Jesus, the Lord changed Simon's name to Cephas, better known to us as Peter. This same Peter walked on water, healed many in the name of Jesus, and preached on the Day of Pentecost. This bold, effective preacher may not have met Jesus if it hadn't been for his brother Andrew.

You may see your life and ministry as miniscule or less important when compared to someone else's. However, you are called for a purpose, so don't neglect what God is telling you to do. Don't see any task from the Lord as "little." And if you don't feel as though you have a task, seek one out. Pray about it. Ask, "Lord what do you want me to do?" You never know if the person God says to talk to in the coffee shop is the next Peter. You never know if your backslidden family member's testimony is going to save hundreds of lives. You never know the potential of the person you are reaching for.

God, I pray that you would use me in whatever way you want. Help me to share your gospel with others. Allow me to be led by the Spirit. And help me to know that your purpose for my life is great.

John 3:3–6
Jesus answered and said unto him, Verily, verily, I say unto thee, Except a man be born again, he cannot see the kingdom of God. Nicodemus saith unto him, How can a man be born when he is old? can he enter the second time into his mother's womb, and be born? Jesus answered, Verily, verily, I say unto thee, Except a man be born of water and of the Spirit, he cannot enter into the kingdom of God. That which is born of the flesh is flesh; and that which is born of the Spirit is spirit.

In John 3, Nicodemus, a ruler of the Jews, came to Jesus by night seeking the Master's knowledge. Jesus, recognizing the nature of this man's veiled request in verse 2, told Nicodemus, "Except a man be born again, he cannot see the kingdom of God." Naturally, Nicodemus was confused and asked how being born again was possible. Jesus answered, "Except a man be born of water and of the Spirit, he cannot enter into the kingdom of God. That which is born of the flesh is flesh; and that which is born of the Spirit is spirit."

This is a powerful lesson: we must be born again in order to enter the kingdom of heaven. The new birth includes being born of the water, which is baptism. Later we will see there is only one way to be water baptized: in the name of Jesus. The new birth also includes being born of the Spirit. In Acts 2, we learn that the way they were born of the Spirit was through the outpouring of the Holy Spirit on the Day of Pentecost, when they spoke with other tongues. The new birth is God's plan; it is the only way to enter into his kingdom.

If you have not been born of water and of the Spirit, pray about it! If you don't understand it, study it and pray that God would give you a revelation. Jesus' words are clear: we must be born again.

Lord, I want to be born again. I will be born of the Spirit through receiving the Holy Ghost and born of the water by being baptized in Jesus' name in obedience to your Word.

John 3:16

For God so loved the world, that he gave his only begotten Son, that whosoever believeth in him should not perish, but have everlasting life.

Jesus Christ came so that we could have everlasting life. We praise him and thank him for faithfully following through with his earthly mission.

Jesus, thank you for loving us, for dwelling among us, and for dying on the cross to give us eternal life.

John 3:30

He must increase, but I must decrease.

These immortal words were spoken by John the Baptist, who knew his mission was to prepare the way for Jesus' ministry. Bible scholars estimate that John preached for about eighteen months before Jesus' public ministry began. Thus, although John's preaching was powerful and effective, there came a day when his ministry began to decrease until it finally ended. It was Jesus' turn to shine.

In order for Jesus to increase, we must decrease—get out of the way by ridding ourselves of fleshly desires and motives. We must understand that without him we are nothing, and without his power working through us, we can accomplish nothing for the kingdom. (See John 15:5.) When we allow him to increase, he can work mightily in us and through us. Ephesians 3:20–21a states, "Now unto him that is able to do exceeding abundantly above all that we ask or think, according to the power that worketh in us, unto him be glory."

Lord, I pray that I would decrease and you would increase so that your mighty power can work through me.

John 4:13–14
Jesus answered and said unto her, Whosoever drinketh of this water shall thirst again: but whosoever drinketh of the water that I shall give him shall never thirst; but the water that I shall give him shall be in him a well of water springing up into everlasting life.

As the disciples were preparing for a journey, Jesus said he wanted to take the route through Samaria—which was highly unusual. Most Jews went out of their way to avoid Samaritan territory. But Jesus had scheduled a divine encounter with a woman of Samaria, and he wasn't about to miss it.

By the end of this divine encounter, Jesus had revealed to the woman that he was the Messiah. This is the first time he openly revealed this to anyone.

Jesus began the encounter by asking the woman for a drink. This surprised her, because a Jew normally wouldn't dream of asking a Samaritan for a drink. But he used this opener to shift the subject from natural water to spiritual water. He said, "If you drink the water from this well, you'll get thirsty again, but if you drink the water I have for you, you will never be thirsty again. My water gives everlasting life."

Jesus is still pouring out that water today through his Spirit. The Holy Ghost still gives everlasting life.

Lord, I ask that you would fill me with the Holy Spirit. Let there be a well springing up inside of me unto everlasting life.

John 4:23–24

But the hour cometh, and now is, when the true worshippers shall worship the Father in spirit and in truth: for the Father seeketh such to worship him. God is a Spirit: and they that worship him must worship him in spirit and in truth.

Worship is essential to humanity. When you look at the entire span of history, man has always found something to worship. Religions have formed across centuries. Even today, people worship celebrities and money.

God is the author and object of true worship, but he is a Spirit, and it is often difficult to worship this being we cannot see. Jesus said that "true worshippers" will worship him in spirit and in truth.

How do we worship the Lord in spirit? Through prayer and praise. How do we worship him in truth? Through studying the Word, obeying it, and living by it.

God, I will worship you in spirit and in truth. I will worship you by praising you with my mouth and by reading and obeying your Word. I worship you!

John 4:35
Say not ye, There are yet four months, and
then cometh harvest? behold, I say unto you,
Lift up your eyes, and look on the fields;
for they are white already to harvest.

Don't wait until you think the time is right for harvest; the world is ripe for harvest right now! Lift up your eyes and look! There are hungry people all around you.

Lord, I will lift up my eyes and look to the fields. Show me where to go to reach hungry people. Help me to recognize there are people who want you right now!

John 5:39

Search the scriptures; for in them ye think ye have eternal life: and they are they which testify of me.

Jesus healed a lame man by the pool of Bethesda. The Jews were angry because this healing took place on the Sabbath. The scene then took on the nature of a court trial when they began to question Jesus about his identity. The more he said, the madder they got. Their rage reached the point where they wanted to kill him because he said that "God was his Father, making himself equal with God" (v. 18).

Jesus appealed to three witnesses to prove his identity: (1) John the Baptist, (2) the works Jesus did through the power of the Spirit, and (3) the Scriptures—because the Scriptures testified of him.

God's Word is revelatory. Just as it revealed the Son, Jesus Christ, it can reveal more to us. As we search the Scriptures, we should pray that God would reveal his truth to us.

Lord, as I search the Scriptures, I pray you would reveal your truth to me.

John 6:15

When Jesus therefore perceived that they would come and take him by force, to make him a king, he departed again into a mountain himself alone.

Jesus had just performed an incredible miracle: he had fed five thousand men plus women and children with five loaves and two fish. To the people, that was one of the greatest miracles he could perform. Free food has always drawn a crowd.

After the people partook of this miracle, they began saying among themselves, "Surely this is the Prophet who is to come into the world" (6:14, NIV).

Jesus perceived they would try to make him king, so he left and went to a mountain alone.

As a man, Jesus was just as subject to temptation as we are. And after this miracle, I imagine he was feeling pretty good. He wasn't alone in the wilderness facing the devil; he had performed this miracle in view of at least ten thousand people. But Jesus wasn't about to let fame deter him from his purpose. He withdrew from the crowd before they could lift him up.

When we are at our lowest in the wilderness, it's easy to cast down pride and serve God. However, after God has just used us mightily, we must beware of pride. Jesus himself showed us what to do. He didn't stay in the limelight very long; he departed and found a place to be alone where he was more focused on his mission than on the people around him. He knew it was not the time for him to be exalted as king.

After God uses you in a mighty way, don't stay in the limelight very long. Find your personal place of relationship where you can be alone and refocus on your mission.

Lord, I will not let pride set in after you have used me in a great way. I will withdraw and go back to my place of personal relationship with you. You are my desire.

John 6:47–48
Verily, verily, I say unto you, He that believeth on me hath everlasting life. I am that bread of life.

Jesus is our everything. We must believe on him. This means obeying what he says and living a lifestyle that is pleasing to him. It means having faith in his Word and his plan for our life.

Lord, I believe in you. I trust you in every area of my life, Jesus.

John 8:7
So when they continued asking him, he lifted up himself, and said unto them, He that is without sin among you, let him first cast a stone at her.

Jesus was the only sinless human to ever walk the Earth, which means he was the only one truly qualified to "cast a stone." Yet he did not. This incident teaches us a valuable principle: do not judge others.

Remember all have sinned and come short of the glory of God, which means we are on the same level as everyone else. We are not qualified to act as judge; only God can judge. It is our job to extend mercy to others as Jesus extended mercy to us.

Lord, I will extend mercy to others as you did to me. I will not judge.

John 8:12

Then spake Jesus again unto them, saying, I am the light of the world: he that followeth me shall not walk in darkness, but shall have the light of life.

Just as the sun is the light of the natural world, Jesus is the light of the spiritual world. If we are walking in his light, we will not walk in the shadowy path of sin, because his light exposes sin. When we walk according to the teachings of his Word, we obtain the light of life.

Lord, I will walk in your light all the days of my life.

John 8:32
And ye shall know the truth,
and the truth shall make you free.

Knowing the truth is to know Jesus and to know his Word, for Jesus said, "I am the truth" and "thy word is truth." Truth is the greatest gift we have. Knowing the truth sets us free from the bondage of sin.

Lord, help me to know the truth—the truth of your Word, and the truth about myself that your Word reveals to me. And I pray that this truth would set me free from every evil in my life.

John 10:1–5
Verily, verily, I say unto you, He that entereth not by the door into the sheepfold, but climbeth up some other way, the same is a thief and a robber. But he that entereth in by the door is the shepherd of the sheep. To him the porter openeth; and the sheep hear

his voice: and he calleth his own sheep by name, and leadeth them out. And when he putteth forth his own sheep, he goeth before them, and the sheep follow him: for they know his voice. And a stranger will they not follow, but will flee from him: for they know not the voice of strangers.

Jesus explained through this parable that there is only one way to him—through the door of the sheepfold. When the Jews didn't grasp the meaning of the parable, Jesus told them plainly, "I am the door of the sheep" (John 10:7).

We can't make up our own version of Christianity or our own way to salvation. We must enter the sheepfold (find salvation) by following our shepherd, Jesus Christ. And those who follow him know his voice.

If a stranger should try to lead us astray, we aren't deceived because we have spent time with our good shepherd, and his voice is the only one we know and follow. He is our Master, and he loves us.

Lord, you are my good shepherd and I will follow your voice. Thank you for leading me, taking care of me, and knowing my name. I will enter the sheepfold your way—through the door. I will not follow the voice of strangers; I will follow only your voice.

John 10:30
I and my Father are one.

In John 10:24 (NLT), unbelieving Jews crowded around Jesus and demanded, "How long are you going to keep us in suspense? If you are the Messiah, tell us plainly."

Jesus replied, "I have already told you and you don't believe me. The proof is the work I do in my Father's name. But you don't believe me because you are not my sheep" (10:25–26, NLT). He went on to say that he knows his sheep, and his sheep know him. They follow his voice, and he gives them eternal life. No one can pluck the sheep out of his hand. Then he drops the bombshell: "I and my Father are one!"

This so infuriated the Jews that they picked up stones to stone him. Jesus said, "At my Father's direction I have done many good works. For which one are you going to stone me?" They replied, "We're stoning you not for any good work, but for blasphemy! You, a mere man, claim to be God" (10:32–33, NLT).

These unbelieving Jews got the point: Jesus was claiming to be God. But they didn't have the revelation; their eyes had not been opened to the truth that Jesus really was Almighty God manifested in flesh.

Here we thank God for the revelation of who he is. We thank Jesus that we know he is the one true and living God.

Jesus, I thank you for the revelation of who you are. You are Almighty God. I praise you, Jesus.

John 12:13

[Much people] took branches of palm trees, and went forth to meet him, and cried, Hosanna: Blessed is the King of Israel that cometh in the name of the Lord.

Jesus is king! Just as they praised him on Palm Sunday, one week before the resurrection, we praise him today. We praise him because he is king in our life, our church, our city, our nation, and our world.

Jesus, you are my king. I give you glory and honor. Your name is great. You are king over all.

John 12:24–26

Verily, verily, I say unto you, Except a corn of wheat fall into the ground and die, it abideth alone: but if it die, it bringeth forth much fruit. He that loveth his life shall lose it; and he that hateth his life in this world shall keep it unto life eternal. If any man serve me, let him follow me; and where I am, there shall also my servant be: if any man serve me, him will my Father honour.

These few verses are packed with meaningful information. First, Jesus, speaking of himself, said that only when a "corn of wheat" falls to the ground and dies can it produce fruit. In other words, life comes by death. This natural-world concept applies to the spiritual world; in order to produce fruit—establish a church—Jesus first had to die and be buried.

According to the gospel (the death, burial, and resurrection of Jesus Christ), we too must lose our life in order to find it. We repent (die out to the world); we are baptized in Jesus' name (buried with him in baptism); and we rise to walk in newness of life (resurrection).

The word "hate" in verse 25 has to do with priorities. "Each believer must establish his or her priorities. We cannot give ourselves fully to this life and yet be committed to the life to come" (Nelson Study Bible). We should be looking forward to life eternal rather than being wrapped up in the pleasures of this world.

Finally, Jesus reiterated that believers must be servants. Servanthood is everything in the kingdom. If you are not a servant, you cannot follow after Christ. I've had friends who were Christians but never grasped the concept of servanthood. It wasn't long before they were walking away from God. Why? Because without servanthood there can be no relationship with him.

Be a servant in whatever you do! Love the things of God. Die to yourself and choose to follow him.

Lord, I want my relationship to be so close to you that your desires become my desires. I will "die out" to this world and live for your kingdom. And I will be a servant to all.

John 13:14–17

If I then, your Lord and Master, have washed your feet; ye also ought to wash one another's feet. For I have given you an example, that ye should do as I have done to you. Verily, verily, I say unto you, The servant is not greater than his lord; neither he that is sent greater than he that sent him. If ye know these things, happy are ye if ye do them.

Here is exciting news! We are servants, and our master is the greatest servant of all. When Peter balked at having Jesus kneel before him and wash his feet, Jesus said, "If I do not wash you, you have no part with Me" (John 13:8, NKJV). Jesus aimed to serve all. That's pretty powerful.

I once heard someone (who did not come from a minister's home) say they were not allowed to sit at the same table as a minister; their sole responsibility was to serve. While it is proper to serve the ministry, it is not Christlike for the ministry to exist solely to be served. Ministers and saints alike must serve others and allow others to serve them.

If you are willing to help others, but have trouble allowing others to help you, bless you, or serve you, then you have a problem that needs to be fixed. Pray about it! Allow Jesus to be your example. You must serve others, but also be willing to be served.

God, I pray that I will be a servant to all, but that I also will allow others to serve me. Help my pride, God. Don't let me think so highly or so lowly of myself that you cannot bless me and use me. I choose to live in your kingdom under your rules.

John 13:34–35

A new commandment I give unto you, That ye love one another; as I have loved you, that ye also love one another. By this shall all men know that ye are my disciples, if ye have love one to another.

The Spirit of God is the most powerful entity in the universe. If you have the Spirit of God living inside of you, then you have the greatest gift on the planet. You are powerful, favored, chosen, and blessed.

My question is, how will people know this? How will your friends at school know that Jesus is living in you? How will your coworkers know you have the gift of the Spirit? Sure, you could tell them. But people don't care about how much you know until they know how much you care.

Jesus knew this long before the book *How to Win Friends and Influence People* was published. He said, "Love people! Because it is by your love for others that the world will know you are my disciples." Not because you can speak in tongues. Not because you can pray with passion. Not even because Jesus has performed miracles through you. It is love. Of course, all the rest will follow. But true disciples of Jesus are those who love others.

Lord, I will follow your example and love others. I pray that people around me would recognize I am a Christian because of my love for them. I pray that my

attitude, my speech, my actions, and my presence will manifest your love. Help me to love as you would.

John 14:6

Jesus saith unto him, I am the way, the truth, and the life: no man cometh unto the Father, but by me.

You can pray this prayer every day.

Lord, I pray that you would be my way, my truth, and my life, that you will lead me in your way, and that I will follow. I pray that I will live out my days in truth. And I pray that you will give me life—physically, spiritually, mentally, and emotionally. In Jesus' name, amen.

John 14:12–14

Verily, verily, I say unto you, He that believeth on me, the works that I do shall he do also; and greater works than these shall he do; because I go unto my Father. And whatsoever ye shall ask in my name, that will I do, that the Father may be glorified in the Son. If ye shall ask any thing in my name, I will do it.

"The works that I do shall he do also." These words of Jesus blow my mind. I believe it happened and will continue to happen exactly as he said. Jesus' disciples went on to duplicate the works of Jesus in healings, raising the dead, opening blind eyes, casting out demons, causing the lame to walk, and so on. They preached all over the then-known world, and thousands of souls were added to the kingdom.

"And greater works than these shall he [the believer] do." If you are a disciple of Jesus, you too have access to all the miracles he did. And greater things! The Greek word for "greater" in verse 12 means to a greater degree or more in quantity. So anything Jesus did, we are going to see happen multiplied times. Believe it! Perform it!

"Whatsoever ye shall ask in my name, that will I do." Anything you ask. You have access to the power of God through prayer. When you ask, you must do it in the name of Jesus and then believe that he will answer your prayer!

God, I believe your Word is true; I will do greater works in your name, and whatever I ask in prayer you will answer. I pray for _____ in your name right now, and I believe you will answer.

John 14:15

If ye love me, keep my commandments.

Plain and simple.

Lord, I love you. I will keep your commandments.

John 14:26–27

But the Comforter, which is the Holy Ghost, whom the Father will send in my name, he shall teach you all things, and bring all things to your remembrance, whatsoever I have said unto you. Peace I leave with you, my peace I give unto you: not as the world giveth, give I unto you. Let not your heart be troubled, neither let it be afraid.

The physical presence of Jesus is no longer with us. But, as John 14:18 promises, he did not leave us comfortless. Soon after his ascension, he sent his Spirit, the Comforter, which is the Holy Ghost, to dwell in us. The Holy Ghost teaches us all things and brings the Scriptures to our remembrance. When we are facing a trial or temptation, the Holy Ghost reminds us who we are in him. He reminds us of our purpose. He gives us wisdom and guidance. And he gives us peace that passes all understanding. We don't have to be worried or afraid when we have the Holy Ghost. He is our comfort, our joy, our guide, and our peace.

Lord, thank you for the Comforter, the Holy Ghost. I pray that your Spirit will be a teacher, a helper, a guide, a comfort, and a peace to me throughout my life. In Jesus' name, amen.

John 15:1–5

I am the true vine, and my Father is the husbandman. Every branch in me that beareth not fruit he taketh away: and every branch that beareth fruit, he purgeth it, that it may bring forth more fruit. Now ye are clean through the word which I have spoken unto you. Abide in me, and I in you. As the branch cannot bear fruit of itself, except it abide in the vine; no more can ye, except ye abide in me. I am the vine, ye are the branches: He that abideth in me, and I in him, the same bringeth forth much fruit: for without me ye can do nothing.

Jesus is the true vine. If you are connected to him, he will produce the fruit of the Spirit in your life: love, joy, peace, patience, kindness, goodness, faithfulness, gentleness, and self-control. If you are lacking in any one of these areas, check your connection to the vine—your relationship with Jesus. Check your prayer time. Because unless you abide in him, you will not produce fruit. To abide in him means to spend time with him. Get connected to the church. Get connected to Jesus Christ.

Branches cannot produce fruit on their own; they must be connected to the vine and the roots. As God's branches, we should be reaching out so we can get other branches "grafted in" or connected to the true vine.

Lord, I will abide in you, in your Word, in prayer, and in your love. I pray that you will produce the fruit of the Spirit in my life, the fruit that brings love, joy, peace, patience, kindness, goodness, faithfulness, gentleness, and self-control. I will abide in you.

John 16:13

Howbeit when he, the Spirit of truth, is come, he will guide you into all truth: for he shall not speak of himself; but whatsoever he shall hear, that shall he speak: and he will shew you things to come.

Jesus promised that the Spirit of truth, the Holy Ghost, will guide us into all truth. We obtain truth through a process of revelation. Think about it. When you first came to God, whether you were born in church or came in at a later time, you knew very little about him. You didn't understand everything that living for God entails. Over time, the Holy Ghost became your guide. Now if you don't understand something in the Word or something your pastor teaches, you pray about it and search the Scriptures for enlightenment.

Let the Holy Ghost be your guide. Seek wise counsel, but learn how the Spirit speaks to you. And, of course, always stay submitted to your pastor and the godly leaders in your life, to the Word of God, and to the Holy Ghost.

Lord, I will let your Spirit guide me into truth. Reveal truth to me in every way.

John 16:23–24
And in that day ye shall ask me nothing. Verily, verily, I say unto you, Whatsoever ye shall ask the Father in my name, he will give it you. Hitherto have ye asked nothing in my name: ask, and ye shall receive, that your joy may be full.

God desires for you to have joy. He said, "Ask anything in my name" so that when you receive it, your joy will be full!

Lord, I will ask things in your name according to your will for my life. Help me to find joy in my prayer.

John 17:11

And now I am no more in the world, but these are in the world, and I come to thee. Holy Father, keep through thine own name those whom thou hast given me, that they may be one, as we are.

Jesus prayed for unity among his followers. We too should pray for unity among disciples (believers). We need unity in our church and with other churches in our city. We have previously covered everything it means to be a disciple of Jesus; now let us pray that we would be unified with others who choose to follow him.

Lord, I pray for unity with other believers. Help me to be unified with the people in my church and in other churches. Give us unity of mind, spirit, and action. In Jesus' name, amen.

John 17:15–19

I pray not that thou shouldest take them out of the world, but that thou shouldest keep them from the evil. They are not of the world, even as I am not of the world. Sanctify them through thy truth: thy word is truth. As thou hast sent me into the world, even so have I also sent them into the world. And for their sakes I sanctify myself, that they also might be sanctified through the truth.

We are in the world, but we are not of the world. This isn't a paradox; it simply means Jesus wants us to live in the world, but to keep ourselves from being stained by the world's evils. We are to stay sanctified through truth, which is the Word of God.

However, don't think that keeping ourselves spotless means we should create a bubble community where no people associated with evil are allowed in. No, that is not God's design. He said, "Even so have I also sent them into the world." We are to go into the world and reach for others. And everywhere we go, we should be shining the light of truth and dispelling the darkness.

God, I pray that you would place me in the world so that I can be your light. Sanctify me and send me.

John 18:36

Jesus answered, My kingdom is not of this world: if my kingdom were of this world, then would my servants fight, that I should not be delivered to the Jews: but now is my kingdom not from hence.

When Jesus was being questioned by Pilate, he responded, "My kingdom is not of this world." Remember this response when you have disagreements with unbelievers. You are a citizen of a heavenly kingdom, and you can't afford to get caught up in things that don't pertain to it. Whether it be politics, debates with coworkers or classmates, government issues, cultural issues, or anything else, you are not of this world's kingdom.

God, help me to remember that I am a part of your kingdom, and your kingdom is not of this world.

John 19:30

When Jesus therefore had received the vinegar, he said, It is finished: and he bowed his head, and gave up the ghost.

The culmination of Jesus' earthly mission took place on Calvary. In prayer, thank Jesus for the blood he shed for you on the cross. Thank him for redeeming you through his death and for taking stripes on his back for your healing. Thank him for loving you enough to die for you. Thank him that he "cancelled the record of charges against [you] and took it away by nailing it to the cross. In this way, he disarmed the spiritual rulers and authorities. He shamed them publicly by his victory over them on the cross" (Colossians 2:14–15, NLT). He accomplished a great work on Calvary!

Jesus, I thank you for everything you did at Calvary.

John 20:25–28

The other disciples therefore said unto him, We have seen the Lord. But he said unto them, Except I shall see in his hands the print of the nails, and put my finger into the print of the nails, and thrust my hand into his side, I will not believe. And after eight days again his disciples were within, and Thomas with them: then came Jesus, the doors being shut, and stood in the midst, and said, Peace be unto you. Then saith he to Thomas, Reach hither thy finger, and behold my hands; and reach hither thy hand, and thrust it into my side: and be not faithless, but believing. And Thomas answered and said unto him, My Lord and my God.

We often refer to Thomas as "doubting Thomas." But there is a valuable nugget in Thomas's request in verse 25. Many people have made similar requests. In fact, there probably have been times when you doubted God's love or miracles or comfort or peace, and had a deep hunger to see or experience those things for yourself.

If you feel your faith wavering, ask God to show up in your life, then reach out and touch him. Experience everything he has to offer, and then you will believe. Once you've had a personal experience with Jesus, you too will exclaim with profound reverence, "My Lord and my God!"

God, I pray for a personal experience with you. I pray that you would allow me to touch you in a way that

I've never experienced before. Show up in my life and increase my faith, Lord.

John 21:15–17

So when they had dined, Jesus saith to Simon Peter, Simon, son of Jonas, lovest thou me more than these? He saith unto him, Yea, Lord; thou knowest that I love thee. He saith unto him, Feed my lambs. He saith to him again the second time, Simon, son of Jonas, lovest thou me? He saith unto him, Yea, Lord; thou knowest that I love thee. He saith unto him, Feed my sheep. He saith unto him the third time, Simon, son of Jonas, lovest thou me? Peter was grieved because he said unto him the third time, Lovest thou me? And he said unto him, Lord, thou knowest all things; thou knowest that I love thee. Jesus saith unto him, Feed my sheep.

After the Resurrection, the disheartened disciples went back to their former occupation: fishing on the Sea of Galilee. They toiled all night but caught nothing. At daybreak, a man called to them from the shore, "Friends, have you caught any fish?"

"No," they replied.

"Try casting your net on the right side of the ship."

They obeyed, and the net was so full they couldn't heave it back into the boat. Peter's heart must have leaped in his chest as he shouted, "It's the Lord!" He jumped into the sea and swam to shore while the others followed in the boat, dragging the net in their wake.

They all ate the breakfast Jesus had prepared, the Jesus asked Peter, "Do you love me?" Peter responded that he did. Jesus said, "Feed my lambs."

Jesus had already made it clear that he was the shepherd and those who followed him were his sheep. By asking Peter to feed his lambs and his sheep (see vv. 15–17), he was asking Peter to watch over, take care of, and feed the followers of Jesus. This is a powerful request: "If you truly love me, take care of others." That must also be our prayer and action.

Lord, you know that I love you. I will feed others the gospel that you have given to me. I will let them know about the relationship they can have with you. I will love others.

John 21:20–22

Then Peter, turning about, seeth the disciple whom Jesus loved following; which also leaned on his breast at supper, and said, Lord, which is he that betrayeth thee? Peter seeing him saith to Jesus, Lord, and what shall this man do? Jesus saith unto him, If I will that he tarry till I come, what is that to thee? follow thou me.

It seems to me that the commission to feed the sheep would be a good place to end the book of John. However, Jesus continued talking to Peter, indicating the manner of Peter's death: "When you are old you will stretch out your hands, and someone else will dress you and lead you where you do not want to go" (21:18, NIV). "Stretch out your hands" likely indicates crucifixion, as early Christian tradition states that Peter was martyred by crucifixion during the reign of Emperor Nero (ca. AD 67).

Glancing over his shoulder, Peter saw John following them and asked, "What about John? Will he die too?"

Jesus replied, "Don't worry about John or any of the others. You follow me."

Each person's journey with God looks a little different, so don't get caught up in what your friend or family member or anybody else is going through. Do not compare your path with someone else's. Your task is simply to follow him.

Lord, I will not compare my struggles, convictions, trials, tests, or mission with others. I will focus on what you have called me to do.

John 21:25
And there are also many other things which Jesus did, the which, if they should be written every one, I suppose that even the world itself could not contain the books that should be written. Amen.

In our final prayer of the Gospels, we thank Jesus for everything he did during his life on Earth. We thank him for the Gospel writers—Matthew, Mark, Luke, and John—and for their faithful testimony of the birth, life, teaching, mission, death, and resurrection of the Lord Jesus.

Thank you, Jesus, for the Gospels. Thank you for coming to Earth as a man and living a selfless life. And thank you that I can take part in your story because you are still alive and working in the lives of your people. Amen.

ACTS

Acts 1:4–8

And, being assembled together with them, commanded them that they should not depart from Jerusalem, but wait for the promise of the Father, which, saith he, ye have heard of me. For John truly baptized with water; but ye shall be baptized with the Holy Ghost not many days hence. When they therefore were come together, they asked of him, saying, Lord, wilt thou at this time restore again the kingdom to Israel? And he said unto them, It is not for you to know the times or the seasons, which the Father hath put in his own power. But ye shall receive power, after that the Holy Ghost is come upon you: and ye shall be witnesses unto me both in Jerusalem, and in all Judaea, and in Samaria, and unto the uttermost part of the earth.

The book of Acts is the first time we see the church in operation after the resurrection of Jesus. Many prayers we pray in Acts will concern the church and our mission today. And it all began with the outpouring of the Holy Ghost. In Jesus' final words in the Luke-Acts volume, he said that when a person receives the baptism of the Holy Ghost, they will receive power to be a witness (Acts 1:8).

We need God's Spirit inside of us because (1) it is essential for salvation (as we will read about in the next chapter of Acts); (2) it generates power inside of us to be a witness. This Holy Ghost power enables a person to speak boldly, to perform miracles, to live right, and to overcome sin. The Holy Ghost is the power of God living inside of you, and it gives you access to the power in the name of Jesus to be a witness for him.

Thus, God's entire plan of salvation revolves around the mission of reaching others. Just as he came to reach others, when we receive his Spirit, it becomes our mission to reach others. So pray! Pray that you would receive that Spirit if you haven't already. Pray that you would recognize and understand the power you have. And pray that his Spirit would lead you to be a witness to those around you—in Jerusalem (your hometown), in Samaria (your region), and to the uttermost part of the earth.

Lord, I pray that as I receive the Holy Spirit I would recognize the power that comes with it. Let me use that power to be an effective witness for you. Whether that means giving me boldness to talk to someone, faith to perform miracles, or power to live a holy life, I will walk in your power. In Jesus' name, amen.

Acts 2:1–4

And when the day of Pentecost was fully come, they were all with one accord in one place. And suddenly there came a sound from heaven as of a rushing mighty wind, and it filled all the house where they were sitting. And there appeared unto them cloven tongues like as of fire, and it sat upon each of them. And they were all filled with the Holy Ghost, and began to speak with other tongues, as the Spirit gave them utterance.

This is the outpouring of the power Jesus foretold in Acts 1. It is the first time the Holy Spirit was poured out on Jesus' disciples. We can learn an important truth from the atmosphere surrounding this initial outpouring of the Spirit.

The Bible says "they were all with one accord in one place"; they were together in unity. They all had the same thing on their mind—being "baptized with the Holy Ghost" (1:5). They were not distracted or at odds with one another; they were focused and unified. This is what led to the climactic moment.

God, I pray that I would be unified with my church. Help us to be focused on the mission you have for us. Let us come together in one place and with one mindset so that your Spirit can move freely among us.

Acts 2:17

And it shall come to pass in the last days, saith God,
I will pour out of my Spirit upon all flesh:
and your sons and your daughters shall prophesy,
and your young men shall see visions,
and your old men shall dream dreams.

We are living in the last days, and God is pouring out his Spirit. Although the promise that we will prophecy, see visions, and dream dreams dates all the way back to the book of Joel (ca. 800–850 BC), we have access to these promises today. Pray for them!

Recently, I wondered about the difference between the young men's visions and the old men's dreams. After some study, I found there was no difference. I felt the Lord was telling me the visions and dreams were both in his plan, and he was revealing that plan in different ways. The young and the old generations often have a different outlook on how to "do" church, how to reach people, and how to execute the mission of God. This is okay; it is actually biblical. The key is bringing the visions and the dreams together in unity.

The good news is that it's the same mission! While God may reveal his mission in different ways to different generations, all of these ways come from God and they all have the same result—the outpouring of God's Spirit upon all flesh.

God, I pray that you would give us visions and dreams of what you want to do through us in these last days. Unify our generations around your plan to pour out your Spirit upon all flesh. And we will prophesy in your name.

Acts 2:37–38

Now when they heard this, they were pricked in their heart, and said unto Peter and to the rest of the apostles, Men and brethren, what shall we do? Then Peter said unto them, Repent, and be baptized every one of you in the name of Jesus Christ for the remission of sins, and ye shall receive the gift of the Holy Ghost. For the promise is unto you, and to your children, and to all that are afar off, even as many as the Lord our God shall call.

This event is the climax of biblical mission. All the Old Testament and the New Testament hinges on this critical moment—the beginning of the church. This passage was part of the message Peter preached on the Day of Pentecost. After the crowd asked, "What shall we do?" (2:37) he used the "keys to the kingdom"

(Matt. 16:18–19) to "unlock" the plan of salvation to the multitude.

This same question is still being asked today. While I've had people ask me this question verbatim, it is often asked through lifestyle. People are searching for something, and as Vesta Mangun said, "Every man has a hole in his heart that can only be filled by the Holy Ghost." We must be ready to show others the answer to their question (Acts 2:38).

Initially, the people who asked that question probably didn't want anything to do with the noisy people pouring out of the upper room. Some in the crowd were "confounded" and "amazed" because they heard these Galileans speaking in their own languages (2:9–11). Some doubted, wondering what it all meant. Others mocked, saying, "These people are drunk!"

But after Peter explained what was happening to them, the crowd asked, "What shall we do?" If you have not repented, been baptized in the name of Jesus, and been filled with the Holy Ghost speaking in other tongues (Acts 2:4), pray about it! Because this promise is for you. It is for everyone.

Lord, help me to understand that repentance, baptism in the name of Jesus, and receiving the Holy Ghost is your plan of salvation, and help me to be ready to stand up like Peter and declare it to others. Remind me that this promise is for me, for everyone I know, and for the whole world.

Acts 2:42–47

And they continued stedfastly in the apostles' doctrine and fellowship, and in breaking of bread, and in prayers. And fear came upon every soul: and many wonders and signs were done by the apostles. And all that believed were together, and had all things common; and sold their possessions and goods, and parted them to all men, as every man had need. And they, continuing daily with one accord in the temple, and breaking bread from house to house, did eat their meat with gladness and singleness of heart, praising God, and having favour with all the people. And the Lord added to the church daily such as should be saved.

Obeying the plan of salvation is not the end of salvation; it is just the beginning. It is your "new birth," your entrance into God's kingdom (John 3).

When runners line up for a race, the official yells, "Ready, set, go!" Similarly, repentance gets us ready, baptism in Jesus' name makes us set, and the infilling of God's Spirit gives us the power to "go." We take off and start running the race with patience and endurance. (See Heb. 12:1, NLT.)

After receiving the Holy Ghost on the Day of Pentecost, the apostles continued: in studying doctrine, in fellowship, in living together in unity, in prayer, and in miracles. They continued daily in the temple and in going from house to house to study together, pray together, and encourage one another. They continued to live with joy and to praise God. And as they continued in these things, the Lord continued to add to the church daily.

Once you fulfill Acts 2:38, you need to continue!

Lord, I will continue praising you, studying, fellowshipping with believers, praying, and seeing

miracles in and around my life. I pray that you would continue to add to the church daily. In Jesus' name, amen.

Acts 3:3–9

Who seeing Peter and John about to go into the temple asked an alms. And Peter, fastening his eyes upon him with John, said, Look on us. And he gave heed unto them, expecting to receive something of them. Then Peter said, Silver and gold have I none; but such as I have give I thee: In the name of Jesus Christ of Nazareth rise up and walk. And he took him by the right hand, and lifted him up: and immediately his feet and ankle bones received strength. And he leaping up stood, and walked, and entered with them into the temple, walking, and leaping, and praising God. And all the people saw him walking and praising God.

Peter and John left the upper room full of Holy Ghost boldness, just as the Lord had said. So whenever the opportunity arose, they used that Holy Ghost power to minister to others.

Verse 4 of this passage has always stood out to me. Peter fastened his eyes on the lame man and told him, "Look on us." Peter and John first focused on what God wanted them to do, then Peter instructed the lame man to focus on them. The man did, expecting to receive something. He didn't realize what it was yet, but he did expect *something*.

This is how miracles are performed. You must first be convinced that you have the power of God and that God wants you to use that power for others. Then, when you see the sick or hurting, focus on them. Focus on what God wants to do through you. Fasten your eyes on them as Peter and John did. Then tell them to focus on you as you lead them to the power of God.

Peter didn't say to the lame man, "Focus on me because I can heal you," but rather, "Focus on me because I am about to exercise the power of Jesus Christ, and *he* will heal you."

I learned how to operate in the gift of faith by watching men like Missionary Charles Robinette and Evangelist Josh Herring. When I was in Haiti, Brother Robinette taught my friends and me how to conduct a "Holy Ghost altar call" and a "miracle altar call." He told us to give clear instruction and be bold in the Spirit. He was showing us the principle that Peter and John and the other disciples had used from the day the church began.

We must expect miracles, and then lead the audience to expect miracles. It works! When you step out in faith, God shows up. Be bold and focus on what he wants to do around you, whether it's preaching, leading in worship, praying in the altar, or talking with a friend, coworker, or stranger who needs healing. God will show up.

I will be bold in my faith, Jesus. I pray that I would focus on what you want to do around me. Let me fasten my eyes on the need you want to heal and then lead others to believe it will take place. And I praise you that it will happen in Jesus' name!

Acts 4:12

Neither is there salvation in any other: for there is none other name under heaven given among men, whereby we must be saved.

I once heard Joel Urshan relate a conversation he had. His Christian friend said to him, "You're one of those Jesus only people, huh?" Joel responded, "No, I'm Jesus everything."

Why do we Apostolics place such emphasis on speaking that name, doing things in Jesus' name, or praying in Jesus' name? Because in Matthew 28:18, Jesus said all power was given unto him. We use that power by speaking the name of Jesus. Philippians 2:10 says that at the name of Jesus every knee will bow. Luke 10:17 says that demons are subject to the name of Jesus. And Acts 4:12 tells us there is no salvation in any other name. *Everything* is in the name of Jesus. So we pray in the name of Jesus.

I will pray for everything in your name, Jesus. I pray over my family, my church, my relationships, my ministry, my finances, and my mind in Jesus' name. I pray for my friends, my city, my country, and this world in Jesus' name. Your name holds all power in heaven and earth, and I am saved through your name.

Acts 4:14

And beholding the man which was healed standing with them, they could say nothing against it.

Understanding this verse will change your perspective on miracles. In Acts 3, Peter and John healed a lame man at the temple gate called Beautiful. It wasn't long before news of the miracle had spread throughout Jerusalem, and Peter and John were rejoicing that so many people believed.

Then the Sanhedrin (the Jewish council) ordered the arrest of Peter and John and had them thrown in jail. The next day, these two apostles were brought before the Sanhedrin for questioning. The council members demanded to know by what name they had performed the miracle. Peter, filled with Holy Ghost boldness, declared it was by the name of Jesus, the man whom the Jews had crucified, but whom God had raised from the dead. Furthermore, no one could be saved except by the power in the name of Jesus!

The council members were amazed at Peter's boldness in expounding the Scriptures, since they perceived the disciples as ordinary men with no formal religious training. The only way to account for the apostles' manner, their bold speech, and their knowledge was that they had been with Jesus.

The Sanhedrin was faced with a dilemma. They couldn't deny that a miracle had taken place; everyone in Jerusalem knew about it. But neither could they tolerate any further uproar over the name of Jesus. They ended up threatening Peter and John, demanding that they and the rest of the apostles not teach or preach in the name of Jesus. This demand had about as much effect as a drop of water in the ocean; multitudes continued to hear the word and believe.

You can spend time conversing or debating with others about God all you want, but if someone sees or receives a miracle, they cannot deny it took place. Seeing a lame man jump out of a wheelchair or a blind man receive sight, or a deaf person begin to hear changes you. When you receive a miracle for yourself, you are never the same.

So pray for a personal miracle. If you are praying that God would reveal himself to a family member or friend, pray that they would experience a miracle. Miracles cannot be denied by those who experience them.

God, I pray for miracles. I pray you would send miracles to those who need a revelation of you. And, Lord, allow me to see miracles take place around me so that my faith in you grows stronger. I receive it in Jesus' name!

Acts 4:29–31

And now, Lord, behold their threatenings: and grant unto thy servants, that with all boldness they may speak thy word, by stretching forth thine hand to heal; and that signs and wonders may be done by the name of thy holy child Jesus.
And when they had prayed, the place was shaken where they were assembled together; and they were all filled with the Holy Ghost, and they spake the word of God with boldness.

Upon receiving threats from the council, the church held a prayer meeting. Did they pray that God would strike the council members dead? No. Did they pray for protection from the enemy? No. Did they ask for favor so the government would give them freedom to preach? Not even that. They prayed for boldness to speak the word of God. They prayed that more miracles would take place in Jesus' name. And when they prayed, the place shook, and they were all filled with the Holy Ghost and went out speaking with greater boldness.

The greatest apostolic revivals (numerically) of the past century were those of Billy Cole and his campaigns in Ethiopia. Hundreds of thousands of people would gather to receive the Spirit of God and experience miracles by the power of the Holy Ghost.

The men and women on his teams were powerful and radical, yet humble. I was told that when these teams got together to pray, they prayed for two things: unity and boldness. They didn't pray for revival or favor or protection. They prayed that the team would be unified and that the team would be bold. This type of prayer will shift cities, countries, and regions. This type of prayer enabled the disciples to turn their world upside down. If you want to be radical, start praying for unity and boldness and watch what God will do through you and your church.

God, I pray that we would be unified around your will and your Spirit. And, Lord, help us to be bold despite everything that's going on around us. Let us be bold with miracles. Let us be bold with speaking your Word.

Acts 5:1–3

But a certain man named Ananias, with Sapphira his wife, sold a possession, and kept back part of the price, his wife also being privy to it, and brought a certain part, and laid it at the apostles' feet. But Peter said, Ananias, why hath Satan filled thine heart to lie to the Holy Ghost, and to keep back part of the price of the land?

Ananias and Sapphira are prime examples of what not to do. They witnessed a Levite named Barnabas bringing to the apostles the money he had received from the sale of a property. Apparently Ananias and Sapphira wanted to experience the same regard of the people as Barnabas had received, so they too sold a piece of property and brought an offering to the apostles. The problem was that they claimed they were donating all of their profits, but they actually had kept some back. Peter proclaimed that Satan had filled their hearts. Their sin was not so much that they gave only a portion to God, but rather that they lied and announced they were giving the full price.

From this we learn not to be fake, not to pretend to be all out for God when we are really holding something back. God knows, and others will eventually find out.

So be true to yourself. If you are going to go all out for God, make that commitment and do it. It would be worse to pretend and lie to the Holy Ghost than it would be to admit your shortcomings and work on them.

Lord, I will be true to myself when serving you. I will not lie about who I am or what I have done. I want to serve you in truth.

Acts 5:12–16

And by the hands of the apostles were many signs and wonders wrought among the people; (and they were all with one accord in Solomon's porch. And of the rest durst no man join himself to them: but the people magnified them. And believers were the more added to the Lord, multitudes both of men and women.) Insomuch that they brought forth the sick into the streets, and laid them on beds and couches, that at the least the shadow of Peter passing by might overshadow some of them. There came also a multitude out of the cities round about unto Jerusalem, bringing sick folks, and them which were vexed with unclean spirits: and they were healed every one.

Acts 5 highlights a great revival in the first-century church. Supernatural things were taking place; miracles were being performed. Everyone was together in unity. The Lord added multitudes of men and women to the church. The sick were healed in the streets. People came from surrounding cities to see the revival. Their faith was so great that even Peter's shadow healed people. It was a spiritual high for the church.

I want that in my church. I want to see everything the early church saw and more. I want revival like this in my city.

Jesus, I pray for miracles, signs, and wonders in my city. I pray that you would add men and women, young and old, rich and poor to your church. I pray for the supernatural to take place. Use me to perform healings of those who are sick. Let my community hear about the things you are doing and come to receive. I am desperate for revival like the first-century church, Jesus.

Acts 5:28–29

Saying, Did not we straitly command you that ye should not teach in this name? and, behold, ye have filled Jerusalem with your doctrine, and intend to bring this man's blood upon us. Then Peter and the other apostles answered and said,
We ought to obey God rather than men.

The apostles filled all of Jerusalem with their doctrine. Imagine if everyone in your community at least heard about the gospel of Jesus Christ—his death, burial, and resurrection—repentance, baptism in the name of Jesus, and the infilling of the Holy Ghost evidenced by speaking in other tongues. The apostles spread this gospel all over their city. How? Verse 29 gives us the answer: They obeyed God.

God, I want to spread your doctrine all over my city. I will obey you, your word, and your commandments.

Acts 5:41–42
And they departed from the presence of the council, rejoicing that they were counted worthy to suffer shame for his name. And daily in the temple, and in every house, they ceased not to teach and preach Jesus Christ.

The apostles rejoiced, met daily, and continued to teach and preach. It was that simple. We can learn a few things from this passage. First, the apostolic church was a happy church. They rejoiced even when trouble came. People want to be a part of rejoicing. God is not somber; he is joyful. Make sure that when you meet, it is a joyful time. Of course, there is a time for weeping and mourning, but overall, the atmosphere should be joyful.

Second, they met daily. I've previously mentioned campus ministry. When we first started, we would meet once a week in an off-campus apartment building. Some of our group would show up, we would have our Bible study, then we would go home. Sometimes a few of us would hang out, but not very often would the whole group get together.

One semester we decided to change that. We went to CMI Awakening Conference together and came back united. From that point on, I made sure we met *every day*. If anyone had lunch on campus, we ate together every day. Mondays we met to hang out or study. Tuesdays we all went out to dinner after church. Wednesdays we played games or studied together in the library. Thursdays we met for prayer either on campus or at the church. Fridays many of us went to help with youth service. Saturdays we hung out, had fun, and attended different events together. Sundays we held service on campus after we all attended our home churches.

It was a lot, but we grew. That semester, more than ten people received the Holy Ghost on campus. We saw miracles take place as a result of our prayers. We saw God work in us and through us. We were no longer just meeting for Bible study. We had become a family, and it worked. While this model is tough to replicate if you are not on a college campus, it is a proven model. From the book of Acts to my own life I can say that meeting daily produces revival.

Finally, they did not stop preaching and teaching Jesus Christ. I don't think there was one service that went by during that time with Illuminate Campus Church that I didn't preach the gospel. I somehow worked the death, burial, and resurrection of Christ into every message. That is the flaw of so many churches. They've figured out the community aspect, but they fail to preach the gospel of Jesus Christ consistently. Having fun is important, but never stop preaching and teaching. In your small groups, talk about the gospel. In your coffee hangouts, talk about the gospel. Meet together to play games, but make sure the gospel is still the center. When you do this, revival will explode in your world.

Lord, I want to be like the first-century church. I will be joyful, meet as often as I can, and talk about your gospel everywhere I go. I will see revival.

Acts 6:3–4

Wherefore, brethren, look ye out among you seven men of honest report, full of the Holy Ghost and wisdom, whom we may appoint over this business. But we will give ourselves continually to prayer, and to the ministry of the word.

In Acts 6, we find the model for choosing leaders in the church. Today many of our churches operate according to the Presbyterian model of church government wherein the local body elects pastors and church leaders. Even if your church is not using that model, you likely will find yourself choosing a leader at some point in your life.

Acts 6 is the model we should follow. Look for men/women who are honest, full of the Holy Ghost, wise, and available to work for the kingdom. This will relieve the senior church leaders of everyday duties so they can give themselves continually to prayer. We should pray that God would give us direction to find and choose these leaders.

Lord, if I am given the opportunity to help choose a leader, I promise to look for someone who is honest, wise, and full of the Holy Ghost. I will take this decision seriously and pray about it to gain your direction.

Acts 7:59–60
And they stoned Stephen, calling upon God,
and saying, Lord Jesus, receive my spirit.
And he kneeled down, and cried with a loud voice,
Lord, lay not this sin to their charge.
And when he had said this, he fell asleep.

Stephen was stoned for preaching the gospel. This doesn't happen in most cultures today, but there are times when it seems as though metaphorical rocks are being thrown at you. You likely have been maligned or mistreated by someone because of what you believe.

In the midst of the beating, Stephen cried out a prayer of forgiveness: "Lay not this sin to their charge." It is significant that Saul, who later became Paul, was present at the stoning of Stephen. Stephen forgave him, and Paul later became the first missionary. Forgiveness is powerful for you and for others.

God, when the world does me wrong, I pray that you will not lay the sin to their charge. Reach someone like Paul out of my hurt.

Acts 8:32–35

The place of the scripture which he read was this, He was led as a sheep to the slaughter; and like a lamb dumb before his shearer, so opened he not his mouth: in his humiliation his judgment was taken away: and who shall declare his generation? for his life is taken from the earth. And the eunuch answered Philip, and said, I pray thee, of whom speaketh the prophet this?

of himself, or of some other man? Then Philip opened his mouth, and began at the same scripture, and preached unto him Jesus.

We enter this scene in the Gaza Desert. The Lord had told Philip to leave a red-hot revival in Samaria and take the desert road. He was trudging along when he encountered a man riding in a chariot. This man, described as an Ethiopian eunuch, was returning home to Ethiopia after a visit to Jerusalem. Philip approached the chariot, began a conversation with the man, and found he was reading a passage from Isaiah 53, a prophecy of Jesus Christ. The eunuch asked, "Who is the prophet writing about—himself or another man?" Philip began to preach to him and subsequently baptized him in the name of Jesus. Let's unpack this story a bit.

First, we must define a eunuch. Through physical alteration, eunuchs were unable to have children. In a culture that was all about family name and family legacy, eunuchs had none. However, they "were regarded as especially trustworthy in the ancient Near East and thus were frequently employed in royal service" (*Holman Bible Dictionary*). This Ethiopian eunuch held an important position in the government of Queen Candace of Ethiopia.

Eunuchs could worship God, but they were not allowed to worship in the temple at Jerusalem. The Ethiopian eunuch was apparently a "God-fearer" (a Gentile who had been drawn to the Jewish religion), for he was returning from Jerusalem where he had gone to worship.

This is the persona of the man we encounter in Acts 8. And we find him reading prophesies concerning Jesus in Isaiah 53. In those days, the Bible was not divided into chapters and verses; the prophecy of Isaiah was a single scroll. Right around the same passage where the eunuch was reading, we find another reference:

> Neither let the son of the stranger, that hath joined himself to the LORD, speak, saying, The LORD hath utterly separated me from his people: neither let the eunuch say, Behold, I am a dry tree. For thus saith the LORD unto the eunuchs that keep my sabbaths, and

choose the things that please me, and take hold of my covenant; even unto them will I give in mine house and within my walls a place and a name better than of sons and of daughters: I will give them an everlasting name, that shall not be cut off. (Isaiah 56:3–5)

The "dry tree" signifies there is no family line. When Christ comes, eunuchs who worship God won't have to worry about a family line because they will be a part of the family and genealogy of Jesus Christ. The Ethiopian eunuch was not allowed to enter the house of God due to his deformity, but the Lord said he would give him a house, a family line, and a name better than sons and daughters. That's when Philip began to preach to him the name of Jesus.

Jesus is an everlasting name, a name that will never be cut off. Regardless of your family situation, your background, or your current predicament, the name of Jesus is for you. It is a name for the outcast, the stranger, and the broken. It is a family like no other. Jesus provides a home for the homeless in spirit. He provides a heritage for those with no heritage. And he provides a name, an identity, and an everlasting promise. How do we receive this name? We find out in the next few verses as Philip baptized the eunuch in the name of Jesus Christ. Baptism gives us a name like no other (Acts 8:36–39).

Lord, I thank you for the heritage, home, and name that you give us through Jesus Christ. Thank you, Jesus, for the revelation of your wonderful name.

Acts 9:11–16

And the Lord said unto him, Arise, and go into the street which is called Straight, and inquire in the house of Judas for one called Saul, of Tarsus: for, behold, he prayeth, and hath seen in a vision a man named Ananias coming in, and putting his hand on him, that he might receive his sight. Then Ananias answered, Lord, I have heard by many of this man, how much evil he hath done to thy saints at Jerusalem: and here he hath authority from the chief priests to bind all that call on thy name. But the Lord said unto him, Go thy way: for he is a chosen vessel unto me, to bear my name before the Gentiles, and kings, and the children of Israel: for I will shew him how great things he must suffer for my name's sake.

Before Paul's conversion he was known as Saul, the persecutor of the church. After his Damascus Road experience with Jesus, the Lord told Ananias to go pray for Saul's healing. Ananias was obviously a little nervous because of Saul's reputation. However, God confirmed that he had chosen this man to do a great work for the kingdom.

Never doubt *what* God says, and never doubt *who* God says. If you feel to go pray for someone, go. Don't let your opinion of that person get in the way of God's opinion. He knows the heart of humanity.

God, I will listen when you tell me to pray for others. I won't let my opinion get in the way.

Acts 10:1–2

There was a certain man in Caesarea called Cornelius, a centurion of the band called the Italian band, a devout man, and one that feared God with all his house, which gave much alms to the people, and prayed to God alway.

Anyone can hear from God. Cornelius shows us how. This Gentile man probably hadn't been brought up to fear and love God. Yet he lived devoutly, he feared God, he gave to others, and he prayed constantly. Cornelius was the gateway for Gentiles (non-Jews) to receive the Holy Ghost. If you want more of God, follow this man's pattern.

Lord, I will live devoutly before you. I and my house will fear and respect you. I will give to others, and I will pray always.

Acts 11:29
Then the disciples, every man according to his ability, determined to send relief unto the brethren which dwelt in Judaea.

Global problems abound. The world always needs relief. Sadly, we can't fix all the problems ourselves, but we can give to others according to our ability. Your ability may be finances, time, or talent. You may be able to provide relief by going. You may be able to provide relief by giving. You may be able to drop everything in life and move to a mission field or partner with UPCI endeavors like Compassion Services International, Reach Out America, or the UPCI Children's Disaster Relief Fund. Ultimately, we can all send up a prayer and provide help according to our ability of time, talent, and treasure.

Lord, I will help provide relief according to my ability.

Acts 12:5

Peter therefore was kept in prison: but prayer was made without ceasing of the church unto God for him.

What can we do when our family or friends are in a bad spot? We can pray. In Peter's case, the Lord sent an angel to the prison in the middle of the night. The angel clapped Peter on the shoulder, woke him up, and said, "Hurry! Get up and get dressed! It's time to get out of here." Peter's chains fell off. Cell doors opened. The main gate swung wide, and Peter found himself standing alone on the street.

Peter wended his way through the city to the home of Mary, the mother of John Mark, where the saints were praying, and he stood there knocking while everyone inside debated if it was really Peter. They thought he might have already been executed. They finally opened the door and were astonished to see Peter—alive and free!

God, I will pray for people who need help. I will keep praying until help arrives.

Acts 13:2–3

As they ministered to the Lord, and fasted, the Holy Ghost said, Separate me Barnabas and Saul for the work whereunto I have called them. And when they had fasted and prayed, and laid their hands on them, they sent them away.

Paul and Barnabas were passionate followers of God who did a great work for the kingdom, but it didn't happen overnight; it took time.

From the time Paul was converted on the Damascus Road in Acts 9 to this point in Acts 13, approximately thirteen years had passed. Immediately after his conversion, Paul spent time in the Arabian Desert in study and prayer before returning to Damascus. He had to leave there for safety's sake, so he went to Jerusalem, but his message was rejected there as well, so "the brethren" (Acts 9:30) sent him back to his hometown of Tarsus in the Province of Cilicia. In Tarsus, Paul studied, taught in the synagogue, and possibly started a church, as the apostles later wrote letters concerning the Gentile believers in "Antioch and Syria and Cilicia" (Acts 15:23).

After several years in Tarsus, Barnabas came looking for Paul and brought him to Antioch, where the two preachers brought vast numbers of Gentiles into the church. Throughout the years between his conversion and the beginning of his first missionary journey, Paul had remained faithful and submitted to the church.

Paul did not split from the church to launch his own ministry. He was submitted to the body of believers. It was not until Acts 13 that Paul and

Barnabas were separated *by the Holy Ghost* to embark on their missionary journey.

Let God decide when your "ministry" will start. Don't try to force something you are not ready for. Instead, study, pray, and witness. Teach Bible studies. Make disciples. Listen to your pastors and elders that pray and fast for you. Be submitted to the church. And through submission you will be sent God's way.

Lord, I pray that you would send me through submission. I will follow my pastor and elders.

Acts 13:9
Then Saul, (who also is called Paul,) filled with the Holy Ghost, set his eyes on him.

The first stop on Paul's first missionary journey was the island of Cyprus. Paul and Barnabas, accompanied by John Mark, evangelized across the island until they came to Paphos, the capital of the island from which Sergius Paulus, the Roman proconsul, ruled. Elymas, a Jewish false prophet and sorcerer, was a member of the proconsul's court, and his knowledge of science and the occult had earned him some influence with the proconsul.

Elymas hated that Sergius Paulus had granted Paul and Barnabas an audience, desiring to hear the Word of God. The sorcerer was afraid that if Paul and Barnabas persuaded Sergius Paulus to become a believer, then he, Elymas, would lose his influence over the proconsul.

Paul had Holy Ghost boldness. He wasn't about to back down to anyone, not even evil sorcerers. He skewered the man with a look of righteous indignation and said, "You son of the devil, full of every sort of deceit and fraud, and enemy of all that is good! Will you never stop perverting the true ways of the Lord? Watch now, for the Lord has laid his hand of punishment upon you, and you will be struck blind" (Acts 13:10–11, NLT). A dark mist covered the sorcerer's eyes, and he groped around for someone to lead him. The proconsul was so astonished at the power of God that he instantly became a believer.

When you are full of the Holy Ghost, you receive power. Let that power be bold in the face of the enemy. Set your eyes on the enemy's territory and claim victory for God's kingdom.

God, I pray that Holy Ghost boldness would be inside of me as it was in the apostle Paul. I will set my eyes on the enemy and speak boldly in the Spirit.

Acts 13:50–52
But the Jews stirred up the devout and honourable women, and the chief men of the city, and raised persecution against Paul and Barnabas, and expelled them out of their coasts. But they shook off the dust of their feet against them, and came unto Iconium. And the disciples were filled with joy, and with the Holy Ghost.

If you attempt to do a work for the Lord, I can promise you that trouble will come. Don't be surprised by it.

Paul and Barnabas experienced trouble almost everywhere they went on their missionary journey. The above passage took place in Antioch of Pisidia (a province of Asia Minor). They spoke in the synagogue on the Sabbath and were invited back the next week. Such a huge crowd gathered to hear them that the rulers of the synagogue got mad and slandered and argued against Paul and Barnabas. The two preachers merely shook the dust off their feet and turned to the Gentiles, who were very eager to hear the Word of the Lord. They didn't let the opposition and rejection deter them in the least. Instead, they continued on to the next city filled with joy.

What happens when you don't let trouble bother you, but rather focus on the victories and the next goal? You are filled with joy!

God, I won't let persecution get me down. I will try my best to shake off any pain that comes because of revival. I will focus on the good things you have done, then I will continue on to what you want me to do next. I pray that through all of this you will fill me with your joy.

Acts 14:9

The same heard Paul speak: who stedfastly beholding him, and perceiving that he had faith to be healed.

Every healing requires faith to be healed. Paul knew this and watched for it as he preached and talked to people. While he was preaching at Lystra, he noticed a crippled man whose expression and manner revealed that he had faith to be healed. Paul interrupted his sermon and cried with a loud voice, "Stand up!" The man leaped to his feet and started walking, something he had never before been able to do.

You can do the same. When you have a conversation with someone and it leads to God, check their response. Some people may be dismissive or uninterested in what you have to say. But others will be intrigued. Some even may be ready for a healing right there. God can heal anytime, anywhere, of any condition. Physical, emotional, and mental healings can take place as you pray. So watch for people with faith.

Lord, I pray that you will lead me to people who believe you can work in their lives. Let me have divine conversations throughout my day.

Acts 16:24–26

Who, having received such a charge, thrust them into the inner prison, and made their feet fast in the stocks. And at midnight Paul and Silas prayed, and sang praises unto God: and the prisoners heard them. And suddenly there was a great earthquake, so that the foundations of the prison were shaken: and immediately all the doors were opened, and every one's bands were loosed.

Paul and Silas singing praises at midnight is one of the most exciting stories of the New Testament. It is a story that gives us hope in our darkest moments.

When you feel like you are in a prison, sing praises. When you feel bound by chains, sing praises. When you feel like your future is lost, sing praises. When it seems like everything is dark, sing praises.

Lord, I will sing praises in the middle of the darkest trials of my life.

Acts 17:6

And when they found them not, they drew Jason and certain brethren unto the rulers of the city, crying, These that have turned the world upside down are come hither also.

The disciples turned their world upside down. Their diligence in spreading the gospel changed the then-known world. Let's pray that we would be a generation that turns our world upside down.

God, I want to turn my world upside down, just as your disciples did in the early church. Help me to be bold and directed by your Spirit.

Acts 17:11

These were more noble than those in Thessalonica, in that they received the word with all readiness of mind, and searched the scriptures daily, whether those things were so.

The Word of God is our first contact to the voice of God. Jesus is the Word, and he speaks to us as we read.

Therefore, aim to search the Scriptures daily with all readiness of mind and pray that God would enlighten your mind.

Jesus, I will search your Word daily. Help me to understand your voice through reading and studying the Bible.

Acts 17:22–23

Then Paul stood in the midst of Mars' hill, and said, Ye men of Athens, I perceive that in all things ye are too superstitious. For as I passed by, and beheld your devotions, I found an altar with this inscription, TO THE UNKNOWN GOD. Whom therefore ye ignorantly worship, him declare I unto you.

I love this story. It is Paul truly becoming all things to all men. He arrived in Athens, one of the strongholds of pagan worship. As he preached in the public square, he was noticed by some philosophers who invited him to a meeting of the Areopagus (the elite council that oversaw various areas of religion and education).

In his sermon, Paul spoke to them on their level by using their language, their culture, their literature, and their understanding. He told them they were "too superstitious" because they had erected a monument to the "unknown god" in case they had inadvertently offended a god by leaving him out.

Paul told them what they really needed was this "unknown God"—Jesus Christ. He declared Jesus in a way they could relate to and understand.

I previously mentioned my encounter on the plane in Peru. (See comments on Luke 4:43.) That encounter felt like a parallel of Paul's experience on Mars' Hill. The principle of addressing people on their own level applies in all areas of preaching/witnessing. One of the scariest things God has ever called me to do was to stand on the street corner of my campus and preach. I would stand there on Ball State's campus for five minutes, dressed in a suit, and project my voice across one of the busiest pedestrian intersections in all of Indiana. During those short five minutes, around five hundred people would walk by and hear me preach. Five minutes later the place would be empty.

God had given me the plan, the time, and the place earlier that summer. I had just come through the greatest season of brokenness I had ever experienced, and only through this brokenness was I able to walk up to that street corner. The closer to the starting date, the more afraid I became. I asked God what he wanted me to say, and he directed me to this passage about Paul on Mars' Hill. It was as though God was telling me, "Preach Me to them in a way they will understand Me."

So in those short five minutes I would preach about the healer, the deliverer, and the Savior. I would tell personal stories of healings I had seen, such as blind eyes being opened and cancers disappearing. I would talk about the deliverer and how I had seen depressed people changed in a moment with Jesus. I shared with them that suicidal people on Ball State's campus were completely transformed when they came to Jesus. Finally, I told them that Jesus could be their Savior. I had seen him save many others on five continents—people from all races and socioeconomic statuses. I would close with a prayer for my campus.

During those eight weeks of preaching on campus at 11:50 AM every Wednesday, I battled fear like I had never felt before. The enemy would try to tell me that I was a fraud. I was preaching healing, deliverance, and salvation while I was still suffering through the aftermath of a great trial. God had not yet fully healed, delivered, or saved me from the situation.

I remember my heart pounding as I would walk up to that intersection, although the people never attacked me or heckled me. I was cussed out a few times, but that was hardly a distraction. It seemed I had more support from the people than hate. The battle was in my mind.

Let me drive this point home. You have a testimony, and through that testimony you can be a light to others. Spreading the gospel isn't just the pastor preaching on a Sunday morning to the church congregation; it's you relating to people, sharing your story, and showing them how Jesus fits into their life. It's you sharing victory, even if you are still in your healing process. It's sharing that God is perfect, even when you are not. It's sharing that he is the healer, even when you are still in the healing process. It's sharing that he is the deliverer, even when you are praying through your anxiety. It's sharing that he is the Savior, even though life is hard some days. Meet people at their needs, and you will find that their needs are often yours as well.

Lord, I want to reach others. I pray that you would show me how to share your gospel in a way that people can relate to. Help me to share my story even when I'm still in the learning process. And through my testimony I pray that you will heal, deliver, and save others—and me as well. In Jesus' name, amen.

Acts 18:26

And he [Apollos] began to speak boldly in the synagogue: whom when Aquila and Priscilla had heard, they took him unto them, and expounded unto him the way of God more perfectly.

Apollos was an amazing preacher. He was an "eloquent man, and mighty in the scriptures . . . fervent in the spirit" (18:24–25). However, he did not know about the baptism of the Holy Ghost or water baptism in the name of Jesus for the remission of sin; he only knew the baptism of John. So when he came to Ephesus, two things happened.

First, after hearing Apollos preach, Aquila and Priscilla took him aside and expounded unto him the way of God more perfectly. They taught him things he did not know. This is like the passionate Christian that comes to your church not knowing the full truth of who Jesus is or about baptism in the Spirit or water baptism in the name of Jesus. Aquila and Priscilla didn't reprimand Apollos or tell him to stop preaching or tell him he was wrong. Instead, they shared the truth more perfectly. That is the first amazing thing that took place.

The second amazing thing was that Apollos listened. He was easily a better preacher than Aquilla and Priscilla. We see later that he was a better orator than Paul himself. He was powerful, electric, and captivating. Apollos could have rebuffed Aquilla and Priscilla. He could have pulled the crowd to his point of view. He could have let his popularity and charisma guide his path. Instead, he allowed these two members of the laity to teach him. And through this,

Apollos was able to preach Jesus Christ in a greater way. This is how the body of Christ is designed to work.

We learn from this example to always be willing to help a passionate Christian understand the Scriptures more clearly. And we learn to always be willing to let a teacher explain to us the Word of God more perfectly.

Lord, I will help others understand your Word more clearly. I will take them aside and teach them without admonishment. And I myself will be teachable. I will not be prideful, but I will submit to others wiser than myself.

Acts 19:2–6
He said unto them, Have ye received the Holy Ghost since ye believed? And they said unto him, We have not so much as heard whether there be any Holy Ghost. And he said unto them, Unto what then were ye baptized? And they said, Unto John's baptism. Then said Paul, John verily baptized with the baptism of repentance, saying unto the people, that they should believe on him which should come after him,

that is, on Christ Jesus. When they heard this, they
were baptized in the name of the Lord Jesus.
And when Paul had laid his hands upon them, the
Holy Ghost came on them; and they spake with
tongues, and prophesied.

Like the previous story with Apollos, these disciples needed to know the full truth. They were believers, but they had never heard about water baptism in Jesus' name or about the infilling of the Holy Ghost. So Paul taught them, rebaptized them, and they were filled with the Holy Ghost.

Look for people who are hungry for the full truth.

God, lead me to people who are hungry for the full truth as outlined your Word.

Acts 19:14–16
And there were seven sons of one Sceva, a Jew, and chief of the priests, which did so. And the evil spirit answered and said, Jesus I know, and Paul I know; but who are ye? And the man in whom the evil spirit was

leaped on them, and overcame them, and prevailed against them, so that they fled out of that house naked and wounded.

These disciples are the opposite of the last two stories. These sons of Sceva knew a little bit—just enough to get them in trouble. They were not subject to a teacher who could have given them a more perfect understanding. Furthermore, it seems they didn't even have a relationship with God because the spirit world didn't know who they were. And it showed. They were attacked and beaten by the enemy.

It is interesting that the Bible presents these three stories in a row: Apollos, a mighty preacher, who submitted to a couple who taught him something he needed to know; a small group of disciples in Ephesus who submitted to Paul, a traveling preacher; and the sons of a prominent Jewish priest in Ephesus who were submitted to no one and were subsequently attacked by the enemy.

Pray that you are submitted to both God and your leaders. They will protect you from evil spirits.

Lord, I don't want to be like the sons of Sceva. I will submit to godly authority no matter how great I think I am. I will listen to my elders.

Acts 20:35
I have shewed you all things, how that so labouring ye ought to support the weak, and to remember the words of the Lord Jesus, how he said, It is more blessed to give than to receive.

It is more blessed to give than to receive. Giving feels good. It is exciting. It is fun. Givers enjoy life when they are blessing others. And God takes note.

Lord, I want to be a giver. Please show me someone I can bless today.

Acts 22:14–15
And he said, The God of our fathers hath chosen thee, that thou shouldest know his will, and see that Just One, and shouldest hear the voice of his mouth. For thou shalt be his witness unto all men of what thou hast seen and heard.

This passage is from Paul's testimony to the Jews as he addressed them from the steps of the Fortress of Antonia. God chose to use Paul in a mighty way. He became the first missionary, a writer of a portion of the New Testament, and a light to the Gentiles. His was a powerful calling. We should desire a powerful calling from God for our own life.

God, call me to do great things for your kingdom. I want to be chosen by you. I want to know your will. I want to see you and hear your voice. I want to be your witness. Choose me, Lord.

Acts 24:16
And herein do I exercise myself, to have always a conscience void of offence toward God, and toward men.

Paul was a troublemaker—in the best of ways. It seemed that everywhere he went arguments and opposition broke out. However, Paul never dwelt on these distractions. Instead, he stayed focused on the mission.

There is a difference between standing up for what is right and having an argumentative spirit. Even in the midst of all the quarreling, Paul said, "I want to always have a good conscience with God and man." He didn't let others offend him. He stayed true to his purpose. He knew there was a greater mission.

Don't get caught up in arguing with others about the gospel. Speak the Word, and don't retaliate if it is rejected. Don't let your good words escalate into something evil. Keep your conscience clear.

Lord, I pray that when I am standing up for you, I will be able to avoid offending someone or being offended by them. I want to keep my conscience clear in the sight of God and man.

Acts 26:2
I think myself happy, king Agrippa, because I shall answer for myself this day before thee touching all the things whereof I am accused of the Jews.

The Jews had threatened Paul's life, so the Roman captain sent him under armed escort to Caesarea to appear before Felix, the Roman governor. Felix, being in no hurry to release Paul, kept him in custody, hoping to receive a bribe from Paul. After two years, Felix was succeeded by Festus.

Paul's audience at the time of his hearing consisted of Festus, King Agrippa and his sister Bernice, a number of chief captains, and many principal men of the city. Paul began his defense, saying, "King Agrippa, I consider myself fortunate to stand before you today as I make my defense against all the accusations of the Jews" (26:2, NIV).

Based off this verse, we pray for opportunities to share the gospel with those in prominent positions. By sharing the Word with these people, an effectual door will open for God's kingdom.

Paul continued his defense by relating the story of his conversion. He said he had come "to turn them from darkness to light, and from the power of Satan unto God, that they may receive forgiveness of sins, and inheritance among them which are sanctified by faith that is in me." He preached a powerful message to Agrippa, knowing the king had knowledge of Jewish history, religion, and culture. The New King James Version renders Acts 26:27–28, "'King Agrippa, do you believe the prophets? I know that you do believe.' Then Agrippa said to Paul, 'You almost persuade me to become a Christian.'"

The opportunities we will receive after praying about this passage are ours to share the Word. It is still up to the individual whether or not they will believe. This meeting with Agrippa opened up the opportunity for Paul to travel to Rome and speak to Caesar, people in Caesar's household (Phil. 4:22), and countless citizens of Rome. Pray for these types of opportunities, and God will supply!

Lord, give me opportunities to speak to those in prominent positions. I pray that doors would open to reach people who have influence in my community. All for the glory of your kingdom.

Acts 27:21–26
But after long abstinence Paul stood forth in the midst of them, and said, Sirs, ye should have hearkened

unto me, and not have loosed from Crete, and to have gained this harm and loss. And now I exhort you to be of good cheer: for there shall be no loss of any man's life among you, but of the ship. For there stood by me this night the angel of God, whose I am, and whom I serve, saying, Fear not, Paul; thou must be brought before Caesar: and, lo, God hath given thee all them that sail with thee. Wherefore, sirs, be of good cheer: for I believe God, that it shall be even as it was told me. Howbeit we must be cast upon a certain island.

Due to Paul's appeal to Caesar, he was a prisoner on a boat bound for Rome. They made it to the southern coast of Crete, where they anchored at Fair Havens. But the centurion favored the port of Phoenix, a place farther along the coastline, to spend the winter. Paul warned the centurion not to set sail, but he didn't listen. Sure enough, the storm struck and blew them off course for days. The sky was so dark they couldn't tell night from day, and they lost all hope of rescue.

After going several days without food, Paul stood before the crew and passengers and said, "Be of good cheer!" They were in the midst of the scariest time in their life. They thought they were about to die. But a man who had a relationship with God got up and said with an upbeat attitude, "I was praying last night and an angel showed up. He told me that we are going to be all right because I have a mission to complete." It turned out the angel was right. Every passenger and every crew member was saved just because Paul was on that boat. Paul was a prisoner, but he became the leader of everyone on that boat in that moment.

You may not have a position or a title, but you are a leader chosen by God. When trouble hits, the world should be looking toward you. Pray for a relationship like Paul had, where God can step in and get the glory through your prayer life.

Jesus, I want to be a leader. I pray for a relationship with you that elevates your kingdom in time of trouble. Let my relationship allow me to help and lead others who are not serving you.

Acts 27:42–44

And the soldiers' counsel was to kill the prisoners, lest any of them should swim out, and escape. But the centurion, willing to save Paul, kept them from their purpose; and commanded that they which could swim should cast themselves first into the sea, and get to land: and the rest, some on boards, and some on broken pieces of the ship. And so it came to pass, that they escaped all safe to land.

They made it! There are times when you feel like you're going to die, but you can make it! As Dory says in *Finding Nemo*, "Just keep swimming!"

In this passage, some of the people swam to the island. Those who couldn't swim latched onto boards and broken pieces of the ship and made it to shore. If you feel as though you can't swim one more inch through these treacherous waters, guess what—you can still make it! Sometimes the best we can do is to grab a board or a broken piece—anything that will keep us afloat.

Every time you feel like quitting, think about the lost that only you can reach. Maybe it's a family member you just can't give up on. Maybe it's a word from God you received five, ten, or twenty years ago. It might be a broken word, but hold on to it because

God's promises are sure. Maybe it's an individual you must hold on to in order to get to your next place in God. Hold on! You can do this. God has a plan for your life. You will get through this storm. Don't ever give up.

I am going to make it, Lord. I'll hold on to whatever I can grab as I go through this storm. I will not give up. Your promises are sure. You have a plan and a mission for my life. I will make it.

Acts 28:3–5
And when Paul had gathered a bundle of sticks, and laid them on the fire, there came a viper out of the heat, and fastened on his hand. And when the barbarians saw the venomous beast hang on his hand, they said among themselves, No doubt this man is a murderer, whom, though he hath escaped the sea, yet vengeance suffereth not to live. And he shook off the beast into the fire, and felt no harm.

It's just like the enemy to attack Paul immediately after God had rescued him from shipwreck. The kind islanders started a bonfire to warm the survivors, and

Paul was helping to gather more sticks. He was laying the sticks on the fire when a snake, driven out by the heat, sank its fangs into Paul's hand. Unperturbed, Paul simply shook the viper off into the fire and kept working.

The spiritual fires we build are called revival. And just like Paul, it seems we get attacked as soon as we start working for God. The attack comes *out of the heat.* It may be an attack from a saint in the church, or a physical ailment, or the enemy coming against our mind. But it always seems to happen in the middle of the hottest part of revival. Just be like Paul. Recognize that no deadly thing is going to hurt you—not a physical snake, and certainly not a spiritual one. Shake that snake off, and it will fall into the fire that you built up.

Lord, when the attack comes, I will shake it off into the fire, then I will keep on doing what you said to do.

Acts 28:20

For this cause therefore have I called for you, to see you, and to speak with you: because that for the hope of Israel I am bound with this chain.

I almost started shouting as I read this verse! Paul had finally reached Rome and was allowed to find lodging, although he was guarded 24/7. He called for the Jews in Rome to visit him so he could get acquainted and explain his situation to them. And this was his statement: "For the hope of Israel I am bound with this chain."

I don't know what chain you are bound by as you read this book, but I do know it will not only work for your good, but for the good of others as well. If you feel bound right now, recognize that your chain is a beacon of hope for others. Chains of depression will become a testimony of liberty. Chains of fear will become a testimony of boldness. Chains of anxiety will become a testimony of joy.

Your chains are a hope for this world because your chains will not stay on you. That trial will not be there forever. Show the world that although you are bound by a chain, you are still a servant of Jesus Christ. The Lord is worthy despite your chain. He is the king despite your hurt. And when the world sees you in chains, still praising, they will receive hope.

Lord, let my chain be a beacon of hope for my world. Let my chain be a testimony for someone else to come out of their situation and serve the God who gives all joy. My chain is hope for the world.

Acts 28:31

Preaching the kingdom of God, and teaching those things which concern the Lord Jesus Christ, with all confidence, no man forbidding him.

The last verse in Acts seems anticlimactic: Paul continued teaching and preaching. The writer didn't continue the story of Paul's ministry. He didn't reveal the nature of Paul's death. The story just kept going. And that is powerful.

Keep on going. Keep preaching. Keep teaching. Keep telling your friends about God. Keep supporting your pastor. Keep teaching Bible studies.

Keep fasting. And keep praying. Until Jesus comes, we will keep on.

Lord, I will keep following your will for my life. I will serve you until the day of your return. I will keep on spreading your gospel with confidence.

www.ingramcontent.com/pod-product-compliance
Lightning Source LLC
Chambersburg PA
CBHW062048080426
42734CB00012B/2584